The Marching Band Handbook

The Marching Band Handbook

Competitions, Instruments, Clinics, Fundraising,
Publicity, Uniforms, Accessories, Trophies,
Drum Corps, Twirling, Color Guard, Indoor Guard,
Music, Travel, Directories, Bibliographies, Index

SECOND EDITION

Compiled by **Kim R. Holston**

McFarland & Company, Inc., Publishers
Jefferson, North Carolina, and London

Cover: Trumpet player Mark Wiening of West Chester, Pa.

British Library Cataloguing-in-Publication data are available

Library of Congress Cataloguing-in-Publication Data

Holston, Kim R., 1948–
    The marching band handbook / compiled by Kim R. Holston. —
2nd
  ed.
      p. cm.
    Includes bibliographical references and index.
    ISBN 0-89950-922-3 (sewn softcover : 55# alk. paper) ∞
    1. Marching bands — Directories. I. Title.
  ML12.H64 1994
  784.8′3′02573 — dc20   93-42227
                                                   CIP
                                                   MN

Manufactured in the United States of America

McFarland & Company, Inc., Publishers
* Box 611, Jefferson, North Carolina 28640*

For two prospective marching activity members,
Michael & Courtney

Acknowledgments

I want to thank the band directors, contest sponsors, music publishers, instrument manufacturers, and association directors who responded to my queries.

For special insights, appreciation goes to Dr. James R. Wells, retired director of the West Chester University Golden Ram Marching Band.

Others who assisted my research were Joan Satchell; Kathy Spicciati; James Feeley; Mark and Eric Wiening; Tina Sizemore; Greg Woodruff; William Davern, past president of the New York Field Band Conference; Mary Pandolfo, Assistant, Marketing and Development, Drum Corps International; Cadets of Bergen County; Meindert Zylstra, Manager, Chatfield Brass Band Music Lending Library; Jeff Roquemore, Zanesville High School (OH) Band Director; Brent Lewis, Downington High School (PA) Band Director; Vern Anderson, Chatfield High School (MN) Band Director; Jack Elgin, Mount Vernon High School Bands (VA) Director; Jennifer Bell, Texas Tech Marching Festival; Jim Conte, Penncrest High School (PA) Band Director; Don Williams, Christiansburg High School (VA) Band; James A. Althouse, Chief Judge, Mid-Atlantic Judges Association; Doug Wilfert, Great Valley High School (PA) Band Director; Gail Schultz, Marketing and Development Director, The Blue Devils Drum & Bugle Corps; Drum Corps Associates; Major Ronald Horton, Fork Union Military Academy; MGySgt Mike Ressler, Chief Librarian, U.S. Marine Band, Washington DC; Lynn Lindstrom, Winter Guard International.

I would also like to thank my wife Nancy for her advice and suggestions.

Contents

Preface

No definitive, book-length history of the marching band has been written, and it would be a challenging project to undertake. The subject is a broad one with a problem of definition. What is a marching band? A traditional brass band may not qualify; the Gilmore/Sousa/Goldman bands, for example, were primarily concert units. Do percussionists and horn players celebrating a triumph in ancient Rome qualify? How about Civil War drummers and buglers? Mummers? For this book a broad definition applies: any group that plays instruments and on numerous occasions marches in a parade or performs in a contest; or color guards and twirlers that perform to music.

Today there are many types of marching units that incorporate music: high school and college marching bands, drum and bugle corps, string bands, twirling units, and indoor color guards. High school bands, if they so choose, compete in parades or in contests each autumn and during spring trips. Most include woodwinds, percussion and brass, with electronic instruments, tympany, gongs and bells often gracing the sidelines. College bands rarely compete but play at football halftime shows, parade and perform exhibitions during high school marching contests. For the past two decades, drum corps—increasingly independent, nonscholastic units relying on brass and percussion—have traveled and competed each spring and summer.

Strangely, all this activity, which involves thousands of participants internationally, goes unnoticed by most of the populace. Much of the public thinks of marching bands exclusively as high school groups and associates them with parades and football halftime shows. This impression is inaccurate, for during the last several decades the marching band "field show" has evolved into an art form. Shows are often designed by a professional clinician—a drill designer—to use the band members, the music, and the field or gymnasium for maximum visual and aural effect. Many bands have formed competition circuits for weekly contests each autumn. This movement continues to grow and—although publicity is often poor—the contests attract more and more spectators and more and more students accompanied by enthusiastic parents and supporters.

Students need not put their instruments, flags, batons, rifles, or sabers aside after Thanksgiving because marching band and its affiliated activities now are active year round. In the winter, color guards ("the sport of the arts") and twirlers participate in gymnasium contests. In the spring, bands participate in a variety of festivals. In the summer, band members join junior drum and bugle corps and travel nationally. Nor need a marching band member retire after college. Senior drum corps are an amalgam of young and old, and instructors in all the activities are in great demand.

There are magazines covering virtually every aspect of the activity, magazines for band directors, drum corps members, judges, and twirlers. Music publishing houses print catalogs especially for marching bands. Books on how to play instruments, how to twirl a baton, or how to write a show are part of the wealth of existing information. Through consolidating and indexing this information, this new edition of *The Marching Band Handbook* aims to provide comprehensive lists for the director, drill designer, booster, and musician—where to buy instruments or batons, spring and fall competition sites, organizations judging twirling or marching contests, fund-raising organizations and ideas, clinic locations, publishers of marching band music, and magazines covering drum corps, twirling or band. The photos sample, in all its variety, the exciting world of the musical marching activity.

Part 1

Clinics and Workshops

A symbiotic relationship can exist between high school bands and drum corps. High school bands located in the vicinity of DCI or DCA drum corps often can obtain brass, percussion and auxiliary unit instruction. In turn, corps recruitment is facilitated.

Music publishers, such as Jenson, publish score paper and other aids for designing field shows and parades.

Clinics and Workshops

1 Alliance Performance Camp
   (flags)
   c/o Todd Chamberlain
   984 Osage Drive
   Henderson KY 42420

2 American Band College
   407 Terrace Street
   Ashland OR 97520

3 Angelo State University Band
   Camp
   Music Department
   Angelo State University
   San Angelo TX 76909-0001

   Arizona State University Band
   Leadership Training *see* Educational Programs

4 Arkansas State University Band
   Auxiliary Camp
   Box 779
   State University AR 72467

   Ball State University Band Leadership Training (Muncie IN) *see* Educational Programs

5 Bands of America Summer Band
   Symposium (Illinois State
   University, Normal IL)
   Bands of America, Inc.
   P.O. Box 665
   Arlington Heights IL 60006

6 Blue Ridge Music Festival
   Office of Summer Programs
   Randolph-Macon Woman's College
   2500 Rivermont Avenue
   Box 856
   Lynchburg VA 24503-1526

7 Bowling Green State University
   Percussion Camp
   Bowling Green State University
   Bowling Green OH 43402

8 Brigham Young University
   Band Leadership Training
   c/o Educational Programs
   1784 Schuylkill Road
   Douglassville PA 19518

9 Camp Crescendo
   P.O. Box 428
   Lebanon Junction KY 40150

10 Camp of the Dells
   c/o National Baton Twirling
   Association
   Box 266
   Janesville WI 53545

11 Carnegie Mellon University
   Department of Music
   Pittsburgh PA 15213-3890

12 Central Connecticut State
   University Summer Program
   1615 Stanley Street
   New Britain CT 06050

13 Central Michigan University
   Marching Band Camp
   College of Extended Learning
   125 Rowe Hall
   Marshall Music
   Mt. Pleasant MI 48859

14 Contemporary Signatures Ltd.
   187 S. Broadway
   S. Nyack NY 10960

15 Dixie Band Camp
   University of Central Arkansas
   201 S. Donaghey Avenue
   UCA Box 4966
   Conway AR 72032
      Flags

16 Domaine Forget Music and
   Dance Academy
   Le Domaine Forget De Charle-
   voix Inc.
   398 Chemin les Bains
   St. Irénée, Quebec

17 Duquesne University
   School of Music
   Duquesne University
   Pittsburgh PA 115219

18 East Texas State University
   Summer Camps
   Department of Music
   East Texas State University
   Commerce TX 75428

19 Eastern Washington University
   Marching Band Workshop
   Music Department MS-100
   Eastern Washington University
   Cheney WA 99004

20 Educational Programs
   1784 West Schuylkill Road
   Douglassville PA 19518
      Sponsors band leadership
      programs

21 Florida A & M University
   Marching 100 Band Camp
   FAMU Box 425
   Martin Luther King, Jr. Blvd.
   Tallahassee FL 32307

22 Florida State University Sum-
   mer Music Camps
   Florida State University
   School of Music R-71
   Tallahassee FL 32306

Furman University Band Leadership Institute *see* Educational
   Programs

George Mason University Band
   Leadership Training *see* Educational Programs

23 George N. Parks Band Leadership Academy
   P.O. Box 6956
   West Palm Beach FL 34405-
   0956

24 George Parks Drum Major
   Academy/Tom Hannum Per-
   cussion Seminar
   University of Alabama
   Box 870368
   Tuscaloosa AL 35487

Georgia Institute of Technology
   see Educational Programs

25 Gila Summer Band and Flag
   Camp
   Western New Mexico University
   P.O. Box 680
   Silver City NM 88062-0680

26 Gila Summer Band Director's
   Workshop
   Western New Mexico University
   P.O. Box 680
   Silver City NM 88062-0680
      Santa Clara Vanguard Drum
      Corps instructs in flags

27 High Plains Band Camp
Department of Music
Fort Hays State University
600 Park Street
Hays KS 67601
Flags

Illinois State University Marching
Band Camp *see* Bands of
America Summer Band Sym-
posium

28 Indiana University Marching
Band and Band Conductors
Workshops
Office of Special Programs
Indiana University
School of Music
Merrill Hall 121
Bloomington IN 47405

29 Indianhead Arts Center Brass/
Woodwind Repair
U.W.-Indianhead Arts Center
Box 315
Shell Lake WI 54871

30 International Music Camp
1725 11th Street SW
Minot ND 58701
Includes: twirling, drumming

31 International Percussion
Workshop
U.M.K.C. Conservatory of
Music
4949 Cherry
Kansas City MO 64110-2499

32 Iowa State University Marching
Band Camp
Reiman Music
Iowa State University
Ames IA 50011

Kent State University *see* Educational Programs (Band Leadership Training); Marching Band
and Band Front Conference
Workshop (color guard)

Lafayette College *see* Marching
Band and Band Front Con-
ference Workshop

33 Lake McDonald Music Centre
C.A.M.M.A.C.
1751 Richardson, #8224
Montreal, Quebec

34 Lutton Music Personnel Service
Inc.
P.O. Box 13985
Gainesville FL 32604

35 Marching Band and Band Front
Conference Workshop
1784 West Schuylkill Road
Douglassville PA 19518
Sites: Kent State University OH
(color guard only); Lafayette
College PA; University of
Maryland, West Chester Uni-
versity PA

36 Memphis State University
Marching Band Camp
Amro Music
Memphis State University
Memphis TN 38163

37 Mid-America Music Camp
1402 M Street
Aurora NE 68818
Site: Grand Isle

38 Mid-Atlantic Band Camp
6219 Lakeside Avenue
Richmond VA 23228
Band Front Camp (Ferrum
VA)

39 Mid-West International Band
and Orchestra Clinic
1502 Huntington Drive
Glenview IL 60025

40 Minnesota Instrumental and
Conducting Symposium
St. Olaf College
1520 St. Olaf Avenue
Northfield MN 55057-1098

41 Music Performance Workshops
505 N. Central Avenue
Laurel DE 19956

42 Nebraska Junior High Music
Camp
Box 234
Malcolm NE 68402

43 New England Music Camp
549 I Spring Street
Manchester CT 06040

44 Oklahoma State University
Drum Major and Flag Camp
Oklahoma State University
Bands
218 Seretean Center for the
Performing Arts
Stillwater OK 74078-0001

45 Oregon State University Music
Camps
Oregon State University
Corvallis OR 97331

46 Personal Advanced Leadership
Training
c/o Educational Resources, Inc.
1784 Schuylkill Road
Douglassville PA 19518

47 Seminar in Computers and
Music Synthesis for Music
Educators
University of Wyoming/Casper
College
125 College Drive
Casper WY 82601

48 Siena Summer Music Institute
595 Prospect Road—U.S. Office
Waterbury CT 06706
Site: Florence, Italy (includes
marching)

49 Skidmore Jazz Institute
Skidmore College

Office of the Dean of Special
Programs
Sarasota Springs NY 12866

50 Smith Walbridge Clinics
11 Magnolia Court
Savoy IL 61874
Site: Champaign-Urbana

51 Sounds of Summer
c/o Yamaha Corporation of
America
3445 East Paris S.E.
Grand Rapids MI 49512
Drum Set Workshop: Tempe
AZ, Boulder CO, Columbus
OH, Denton TX; Marching
Band Camp: Thornton CO,
Wichita KS, College Park MD,
Grand Rapids MI, Mt. Pleas-
ant MI, Easton PA, West
Chester PA, Vermillion SD;
Marching Percussion Camp:
Phoenix AZ, Tucson AZ,
Santa Barbara CA, Gainesville
FL, Valdosta GA, Atlanta GA,
Itasca IL, Ames IA, Iowa City
IA, Port Huron MI, Minne-
apolis MN, Kearney NE, Las
Vegas NV, Greenville NC,
International Peace Garden
ND, Columbus OH, Bowling
Green OH, Shawnee OK,
Memphis TN, Nacogdoches
TX, San Marcos TX, San An-
tonio TX, El Paso TX, Wichita
Falls TX, Odessa TX, Ellens-
burg WA, Madison WI

52 Southeast Summer Music
Camps
One University Plaza
Southeast Missouri State
University
Cape Girardeau MO 63701-4799

53 Southwest Texas State University Marching Camp
Southwest Texas State University
San Marcos TX 78666

54 Southwestern Oklahoma State
   University Marching Aux-
   iliary Camp
   Southwestern Oklahoma State
   University
   Department of Music
   100 Campus Drive
   Weatherford OK 73096-3001

55 Summer Band Camp at James
   Madison University
   Music Department
   James Madison University
   Harrisonburg VA 22807-0001

56 Summer Workshop Program
   School of Music
   University of South Carolina
   Columbia SC 29208-0001
      Directors

57 Tahkodah Music Camp
   Harding University
   Box 767
   Searcy AR 72149

58 Texas Christian University Band
   Summer Music Institute
   Texas Christian University
   Box 32927
   Fort Worth TX 76129-0001

59 Texas Tech Band/Orchestra
   Camp
   Box 42033
   School of Music
   Texas Tech University
   Lubbock TX 79409

60 Thousand Hills Summer Youth
   Music Camps
   Northeast Missouri State
   University
   Kirksville MO 63501

61 Tigerland Auxiliary Camp
   Summer Music Camps
   Department of Bands
   Louisiana State University
   Baton Rouge LA 70803-0001

62 Tim Lautzenheiser: The Art of
   Successful Teaching
   Office of Extended Education
   Texas Christian University
   Box 32927
   Fort Worth TX 76129-0001

63 Trombone Workshop
   School of Music
   Western Michigan University
   Kalamazoo MI 49008

64 United States Percussion Camp
   Eastern Music Camp
   Eastern Illinois University
   Charleston IL 61920

65 University of Akron
   School of Music
   University of Akron
   Akron OH 44325-0001
      Includes: Brass Performance
      Techniques, High School
      Marching Percussion Camp,
      Junior High School Band
      Camp, Techniques in March-
      ing Band (directors)

66 University of Florida Marching
   Band Camp
   Band Central Station
   University of Florida
   Gainesville FL 32611

67 University of Georgia Auxiliary
   and Drum Major Camp
   School of Music
   Fine Arts Building
   University of Georgia
   Athens GA 30602

University of Houston Band
   Leadership Training see Educational Programs

68 University of Iowa Marching
   Band Camp
   West Music
   University of Iowa
   Iowa City IA 52242-0001

69 University of Kentucky Marching Band Auxiliaries and Percussion Camp
University of Kentucky Band Office
105 Fine Arts
Lexington KY 40506-0001

University of Maryland *see* Marching Band and Band Front Conference Workshop

70 University of Miami
School of Music
Box 248165
Coral Gables FL 33124
Includes: Band Workshop, Marching Percussion, Color Guard, Drum Major, Computer Applications in Music Education

71 University of Nebraska–Lincoln Marching Summer Marching Camp
University of Nebraska
113 Westbrook Music Building
Lincoln NE 68588-0001

72 University of Nebraska–Omaha Summer Flag Camp
U.N.O. Bands, Room 215
PAC University of Nebraska at Omaha
Omaha NE 681182-0001

73 University of New Hampshire Summer Youth Music School
University of New Hampshire
Department of Music, PCAC
Durham NH 03824-3545

74 University of North Texas Advanced Flute Masterclass in Repertoire and Performance Techniques
P.O. Box 13887
Denton TX 76203-6797

University of Northern Arizona Band Leadership Institute *see* Educational Programs

University of Northern Colorado Band Leadership Training *see* Educational Programs

75 University of Oregon Marching Percussion Camp
Oregon Summer Music Institute
School of Music
University of Oregon
Eugene OR 97403
Includes: Alan Keown Marching Percussion Camp, Drum Major/Leadership Camp

76 University of South Carolina
School of Music
Columbia SC 29208-0001

77 University of South Dakota Corps Style Marching Camp and Workshop
Department of Music
University of South Dakota
Vermillion SD 57069-2390

78 University of Southern Mississippi Summer Camps
University Bands
Southern Station Box 5032
Hattiesburg MS 39406

79 University of Southwestern Louisiana Color Guard, Percussion and Drum Major Camps
School of Music
University of Southwestern Louisiana
P.O. Drawer 41207
Lafayette LA 70504-0400

80 University of Texas Marching Band Auxiliary Camp
Department of Music
Box 19105
Arlington TX 76019-0001

81 University of Washington Summer Program
Office of Graduate and Undergraduate Advising
University of Washington
School of Music, DN-10
Seattle WA 98195

82 University of Wisconsin–Green Bay Marching Band Camps
Department of Music
University of Wisconsin
Green Bay WI 54301

83 Valley Forge Military Band Camp
Director of Admissions
Valley Forge Military Academy
1001 Eagle Road
Wayne PA 19087-3695

84 VanderCook College of Music
M.E.C.A. Program
3209 S. Michigan Avenue
Chicago IL 60616-3886

85 Villanova University – M.E.C.A. Program
Music Activities–M.E.C.A. Program
St. Mary's Hall, First Floor
Villanova University
Villanova PA 19085-1699
Directors

West Chester University *see* Marching Band Front Conference Workshop

86 Western Illinois University Summer Music Camps
Western Illinois University
Macomb IL 61455

87 Wichita State University Marching Band Camp
Starkey Music
Wichita State University
Wichita KS 67208

Products, Aids and Software

88 Advantage Showare
239 Southland Drive, Suite B
Lexington KY 40503
Drill design software

89 Alfred Publishing Company
P.O. Box 10003
Van Nuys CA 91410

90 BVP Marching Videos
790 W. Main Street
Newark OH 43055
Videos of marching band contests

91 Coda Music Software
Wenger Music Learning Division
1401 E. 79th Street
Minneapolis MN 55425-1126

92 COHO Company
2904 Branch Hollow
Flower Mound TX 75028
Video for trombone student

Columbia Pictures Publications *see* CPP/Belwin, Inc.

93 CPP/Belwin, Inc.
15800 Northwest 48th Avenue
P.O. Box 4340
Miami FL 33014
Marching band, rifles and flags video tapes

DCI Music Video *see* CPP/Belwin, Inc.

United States Marine Corps Band, Albany, Georgia.

94 DCI Recordings
P.O. Box 548
Lombard IL 60148
    Compact discs and audio cassettes of drum corps shows

95 Dr. T's
220 Boylston Street
Chestnutt Hill MA 02167
    Publishes software

96 Drum Corps Management
    System
JTD Software System
P.O. Box 70553
Sunnyvale CA 94086

97 800 Video Express, Inc.
P.O. Box 142
Palatine IL 60078
    Drum corps shows

98 Electronic Arts
1820 Gateway Drive
San Mateo CA 94404
    Publishes software

99 Lutton Music Personnel Service, Inc.
P.O. Box 13985
Gainesville FL 32604

MacDrums *see* Coda Music
Software

100 Maestro Music, Inc.
2403 San Mateo N.E., Suite
P-12
Albuquerque NM 87110
    Publishes software

101 Maximum Management
P.O. Box 741
Rockville Centre NY 11571
    Publishes software

102 Music Systems for Learning,
    Inc.
311 E. 38th Street, Suite 20C
New York NY 10016

103 National Institute of Music in
    Motion
P.O. Box 789
Plainville CT 06062

104 Opcode
     1024 Hamilton Court
     Menlo Park CA 94025
     Publishes software

105 Passport Designs
     625 Miramontes Street, Suite
     103
     Half Moon Bay CA 94019
     Publishes software

106 Peterson Electro-Musical
     Products, Inc.
     11601 South Mayfield Avenue
     Worth IL 60482
     Strobe tuners/ear training
     devices

107 Resonate
     P.O. Box 996
     Menlo Park CA 94026
     Publishes software

108 RolandCorp US
     7200 Dominion Circle
     Los Angeles CA 90040
     Publishes software

109 Silver Burdett & Ginn
     250 James Street
     Morristown NJ 07960
     Publishes software

110 Take Care
     P.O. Box 73266
     Puyallup WA 98373
     Music care and maintenance
     videos

111 TOA Electronics, Inc.
     480 Carlton Court
     South San Francisco CA 94080

112 Yamaha Band Student
     Yamaha Corporation of
     America
     Band & Orchestral Division
     Alfred Publishing Company,
     Inc.
     P.O. Box 10003
     Van Nuys CA 91410-0003

University of Massachusetts Marching Band, Amherst, Massachusetts.

Associations

113 American Bandmasters
    Association
    110 Wyanoke Drive
    San Antonio TX 78209

114 American School Band Direc-
    tors' Association
    P.O. Box 146
    Otsego MI 49078

115 Canadian Band Association
    Box 5005
    Red Deer, Alberta

116 College Band Directors Na-
    tional Association
    Box 8028
    Austin TX 78767

117 Music Educators National
    Conference
    1902 Association Drive
    Reston VA 22091

118 Music Teachers National
    Association
    617 Vine Street, Suite 1432
    Cincinnati OH 45215

119 National Band Association
    P.O. Box 121292
    Nashville TN 37212

120 National Catholic Band-
    masters' Association
    Box 1023
    Notre Dame IN 46556

121 Women Band Directors Na-
    tional Association
    6954 Garland Avenue
    Baker LA 70714

Selected Bibliography

Articles

122 Bailey, Wayne A. "Marching Tips for the Small Band." *Instrumentalist* (June 1982): 12.

123 Berg, Ron. "Fit to March." *Music Educators Journal* (May 1981): 44–45.

124 Cappio, Arthur L. "Marching Percussion Drum Corps Style." *School Musician, Director & Teacher* (August/September 1977): 62, 65.

125 Dvorak, Raymond. "Marching Maneuvers: Music and Pageantry." *Instrumentalist* (September-October 1946): 6–7.

126 Dye, Ken. "Marching Band Films and Tapes." *Instrumentalist* (October 1980): 96–99.

127 Farnsworth, Roger W. "A 'Do-It-Yourself' Summer Music Camp for Your Entire Organization." *School Musician, Director & Teacher* (March 1978): 50–51.

128 Follett, Richard J. "The Drum Major Camp." *Instrumentalist* (March 1978): 40–43.

129 Green, Gary, and Cury, Donald E. "The Percussion Session Field Solo." *School Musician, Director & Teacher* (May 1981): 12–14.

130 Hammer, Rusty. "From Battlefield to Concert Hall: The Career of Patrick S. Gilmore." *Instrumentalist* (June 1992): 46–47, 49.

131 Hejl, James G. "Marching Band Warm-Ups." *Instrumentalist* (August 1983): 26–28.

132 Holmes, Charles. "Snare Drum Tips." *Instrumentalist* (August 1987): 48, 50, 52.

133 Holston, Kim. "West Chester, Pennsylvania: A Lively Place for Marching." *Music and Pageantry Journal* (January 1982): 23.

134 Hong, Sherman. "Common Sense in Marching Percussion." *Percussive Notes* (Spring/Summer 1980): 42–45.

135 _____. "Judging Marching Percussion." *Instrumentalist* (September 1989): 44, 46, 48.

136 Lange, Sam. "Sam Lange Talks About Drum Majoring and Field Generalship." *Drum Major* (January 1982): 8.

137 Lautzenheiser, Tim. "Today's Marching Band Percussion Section." *School Musician, Director & Teacher* (August/September 1980): 14–16.

138 LeCroy, Hoyt F. "Section Solos for the Marching Percussion Section." *School Musician, Director & Teacher* (April 1979): 48, 67.

139 Mahin, Bruce P. "Business Uses of Computers." *Instrumentalist* (February 1987): 52, 54, 56.

140 Mallen, James K. "Arranging Rudimental Training Technique." *Percussive Notes* (Fall 1980): 44–45.

141 Mazur, Ken. "Advanced Rudimental Training Technique." *Percussive Notes* (Spring/Summer 1980): 45–49.

142 Michalski, Stanley, Jr. "The Upcoming Gridiron Extravaganza (A Band Director's Comments and Laments)." *School Musician, Director & Teacher* (June 1984): 8–9.

143 Miller, Richard A. "Intensity Designs: Guidelines for Show Planning." *Instrumentalist* (June 1984): 14–15.

144 Montgomery, Timothy. "The Rotation Concept." *Instrumentalist* (June 1981): 10–13.

145 Neiman, Marcus. "If You Can't Find It — Write It!" *Instrumentalist* (September 1987): 80, 82.

146 Nelson, Judy Ruppel. "Gene Thrailkill — Guiding the Pride." [University of Oklahoma] *Instrumentalist* (September 1987): 16–19.

147 Pratt, Stephen W. "The Music Newsletter: An Effective Tool for Music Education." *Instrumentalist* (September 1987): 106, 108.

148 Province, Martin. "Marching Band Warm-Ups for Stiff Chops." *Instrumentalist* (August 1988): 18–20.

149 Rideout, Roger R. "Summer Tasks for the First-Year Band Director." *Instrumentalist* (July 1987): 50, 52, 54.

150 Schoettle, David Allen. "Composing on a Computer." *Flute Talk* (September 1992): 21–23.

151 Smith, Joseph T. "Time-Saving Techniques for the Marching Band Rehearsal." *Instrumentalist* (October 1979): 20–21.

152 Thulien, James W. "So Now You Want to March Corps Style?" *School Musician, Director & Teacher* (May 1980): 10–11.

153 Trytten, Kim. "The Benefits of Marching Camp." *Instrumentalist* (June 1993): 33–34, 36, 38, 40.

154 Vogel, Lauren. "Marching Mallet Percussion." *Instrumentalist* (May 1981): 48–51.

155 Wanamaker, Jay A. "Visual Effects." *Percussive Notes* (Fall 1979): 46.

Books

156 Bennett, George T. *The In and Out of 26 Letter Formations.* Marching Maneuver Series, Vol. IX. Chicago IL: Gamble Hinged Music Company, 1939.

157 _____. *New and Novel Formations for Marching Bands and Drum Corps.* Marching Maneuver Series, Vol. VII. Chicago IL: Gamble Hinged Music Company, 1938.

158 Butts, Carrol M. *High School Band Clinic: Drills & Exercises That Improve Performance.* Englewood Cliffs NJ: Prentice-Hall, 1978.

159 *Camp Kit.* Colgate WI (631 Violet CT 53017).

160 Casavant, Albert R. *Block Formation Drill.* San Antonio TX: Southern Music Company, n.d.

161 _____. *Block Progressions.* San Antonio TX: Southern Music Company, 1965.

162 _____. *Block Specials.* San Antonio TX: Southern Music Company, 1968.

163 _____. *Corner Drill Movements.* San Antonio TX: Southern Music Company, 1967.

164 _____. *Double Gait.* San Antonio TX: Southern Music Company, 1968.

165 _____. *The Fast Break.* San Antonio TX: Southern Music Company, 1962.

166 _____. *Field Entrances.* San Antonio TX: Southern Music Company, 1959.

167 _____. *Field Routines: Book 1: Five Complete Precision Drill Routines with Suggested Music.* Grade 3. For: Football Halftime, Field Exhibition, Marching Contest. San Antonio TX: Southern Music Company, n.d.

168 _____. *Manual of Drill.* San Antonio TX: Southern Music Company, 1960.

169 _____. *Marching Routines.* 2 v. Book 1: Five Complete Precision Drill Field Routines (Grade 1) Company Front Drill, End Zone Entrances and Exits, 1963. Book 2: Five Precision Drill Routines with Company Front End Zone and Side Entrances and Exits (Grade 1), 1964. San Antonio TX: Southern Music Company, 1963-64.

170 _____. *Phalanx Drill Movements.* San Antonio TX: Southern Music Company, 1959.

171 _____. *Precision Drill.* San Antonio TX: Southern Music Company, 1957.

172 _____. *Precision Drill Line Movements.* San Antonio TX: Southern Music Company, 1958.

173 _____. *The Precision Drill Squad.* San Antonio TX: Southern Music Company, 1960.

North Penn High School Marching Knights, Lansdale, Pennsylvania.

174 _____. *The Precision Drill Team.* San Antonio TX: Southern Music Company, 1961.

175 _____. *Precision Flash.* San Antonio TX: Southern Music Company, 1962.

176 _____. *Progression Drill Line Movements.* San Antonio TX: Southern Music Company, 1963.

177 _____. *Rhythmic Arm Movements for Marching.* San Antonio TX: Southern Music Company, 1962.

178 _____. *Six to Five.* San Antonio TX: Southern Music Company, 1962.

179 _____. *Staggered Block Drill Movements.* San Antonio TX: Southern Music Company, 1968.

180 _____. *Wrapping the Block.* San Antonio TX: Southern Music Company, 1968.

181 Dale, Carroll R. *Fundamentals of Drill.* Chicago IL: Gamble Hinged Music Company, 1940.

182 Foster, Robert E. *Multiple-Option Marching Band Techniques.* 3rd ed. Van Nuys CA: Alfred Publishing Company, 1991.

183   Garofalo, Robert. *Blueprint for Band: A Guide to Teaching Comprehensive Musicianship Through School Band Performance.* Portland ME: J. Weston Walch, 1976.

184   Glasgow, William. *Exhibition Drills.* Harrisburg PA: Military Service Publishing Company, 1958.

185   Hal Leonard Music. *Band Shows Can Be Easy.* Winona MN, 1948.

186   Hindsley, Mark H. *Band-at-ten-tion! A Manual for the Marching Band.* Drill masters and drum majors ed. New York: Remick Music Corporation, 1932.

187   _____. *How to Twirl a Baton.* Chicago IL: Ludwig and Ludwig, 1928.

188   _____. *24 Formations, Designs, and Entrances for the Marching Band.* Marching Maneuver Series, Vol. I. Chicago IL: Gamble Hinged Music Company, 1935.

189   Hopper, Dale. *Corps Style Marching.* Oskaloosa IA: C.L. Barnhouse, 1977.

190   _____. *The Drill Designers' Idea Book.* Macomb IL: Dale Hopper Music, 1988.

191   Jones, Stefan. *Band Shows Dance Drill Book.* New York NY: Charles H. Hansen Music Corporation, 1953.

192   Lee, Jack. *Modern Marching Band Techniques.* Winona MN: Hal Leonard Music Company, 1955.

193   Lentz, Bernard. *Cadence System of Teaching Close Order Drill and Exhibition Drills.* 8th ed. Harrisburg PA: Military Service Publishing Company, 1957.

194   Long, A.H. *Marching to the Yard Lines.* Ponca City OK: Luther Music Company, 1952.

195   Lyon, Muriel J., and Peterson, Marcia M. *Fundamental Drill Team and Marching Percussion.* Dubuque IA: William C. Brown, 1964.

196   Mahan, Jack. *Quick Steps to Marching.* New York: Carl Fischer, 1953.

197   Malstrom, George N. *The Drum Major's Manual.* Chicago IL: Ludwig and Ludwig, 1928.

198   Marcouiller, Don R. *Marching for Marching Bands.* Dubuque IA: William C. Brown, 1958.

199 Meaux, Robert. *Contemporary Field Designs for Marching Band.* San Antonio TX: Southern Music Company, 1990.

200 Oldfield, Willis P. *Twenty and Seven Drill Band Maneuvers.* Mansfield PA: Swain's Music House, 1938.

201 *Opportunities in Music Careers 1991.* Saddle Brook NJ: Regent Book Company, Wholesale Booksellers (101A Route 46, 07662). $10.95.

202 Parks, George. *The Dynamic Drum Major.* Oskaloosa IA: C.L. Barnhouse, 1984.

203 Raxsdale, Bill. *Contemporary Color Guard Manual.* New Berlin WI: Jenson Publications, 1980.

204 Regent Book Company. *Opportunities in Music Careers 1991.* Saddle Brook, NJ.

205 Revelli, William D., and Cavender, George. *Marching Fundamentals and Techniques for the School Bandsman.* Ann Arbor MI: LesStrang Publishing Company, 1961.

206 Reynolds, R.B. *Drill and Evolutions of the Band.* Annapolis MD: National Service Publishing Company, 1928.

207 Schilling, Richard Lee. *Marching Band Maneuvers.* Evanston IL: Instrumentalist Company, 1961.

208 Shellahamer, Bentley; Swearingen, James; and Woods, Jon. *The Marching Band Program: Principles and Practices.* Oskaloosa IA: C.L. Barnhouse, 1986.

209 Smith, Claude B., and Capel, Wallace. *Practical Stunts and Evolutions.* Marching Maneuver Series, Vol. II. Chicago IL: Gamble Hinged Music Company, 1935.

210 Snider, Larry. *Developing the Corps Style Percussion Section.* Oskaloosa IA: C.L. Barnhouse, 1979.

211 _____. *Total Marching Percussion.* Oskaloosa IA: C.L. Barnhouse. Book 1: 1976. Book 2: 1978. Book 3: 1983.

212 Weaver, Max, and Butts, Carrol M. *Field-Color Entrances for Marching Band.* Oskaloosa IA: C.L. Barnhouse, 1975.

213 _____ and _____. *Field-Color Shows for Marching Band.* Oskaloosa IA: C.L. Barnhouse, 1979.

214 West, Adam. *Marching Class Method.* San Antonio TX: Southern Music Company, 1953.

215 World Rhythm. *Mastering the Rudiments.* Colorado Springs CO, 1993.

216 Wright, Al G. *Marching Band Fundamentals.* New York: Carl Fischer, 1963.

217 _____. *The Show Band.* Evanston IL: Instrumentalist Company, 1957.

218 Wyand, Alan. *Band Training Camps.* York PA, 1962.

Part 2

Competitions

General

To compete or not to compete? The question has perplexed directors for half a century. Even though they recognize the public relations importance of a marching band, some feel contests or even football halftime shows debilitate concert band and orchestras. Nevertheless, schools with the best marching bands usually have the best indoor ensembles. As Paul Dobson, Jr., director of bands at Hardee County Junior High School in Wauchula, Florida, said, "So what if it [marching band] is not the greatest single achievement of musical development in history? The kids love it, and I love to watch them as they develop and succeed. 'Ten-hut!'" (in "Marching Bands at the Middle School Level?" Music Educators Journal, *October 1990, p. 48).*

Before engaging in competition, questions must be asked. Will the unit be traveling far afield? Outside the country? Outside the state? Saturday or Sunday? Who will provide and pay for buses—the school administration or the boosters? Do the students want to compete every Saturday night in addition to performing Saturday afternoon at a football game? Will they engage in all the practices necessary to achieve a kind of perfection? Will there be a rooting section on the road? Will it be only the hardcore boosters or all *the parents? Publicity—letting the parents know what they and their students will get out of competing—is a high priority.*

It is often easier to win away from home, especially if your region has an established competition circuit. There are probably more bands in the circuit than will be encountered on a springtime trip. Of course, if you have good musicians and a 190-member unit, you may do well. On the other hand, even a large unit may need some experience in the circuit. Do not expect to win the championships the first year.

That first season it may be wise to keep a light competition schedule. Traveling 40, 60 or 80 miles away every Saturday night may exhaust everyone, especially if you don't do well. Winning, obviously, will make the excursions seem shorter. A reasonable policy is to shoot for more points each outing. Even if you don't win, you will have improved—and there's the proof on the score sheet.

Be sure you know the rules for competing in the championships. You may not qualify. Case in point: a band director, dissatisfied with average showings in his circuit, begins a new season in a different circuit. The band does fairly well but must travel to the next state for wide exposure. Then come the area playoffs. The band must win its area playoff to compete in the championships. The trouble is, the band from this area that must be beaten is the perennial winner of not only the area but the championships as well! The new band does not overcome this handicap and thus does not attend the championships. If the band had remained in the other circuit, it would not have encountered this situation because every member band that chooses may compete in the finals. Note that membership in one contest circuit does not prevent membership in other circuits nor the remittance of a small fee to compete in one contest.

Because you will be competing for trophies, rarely money, funding is important. Some competition associations provide travel reimbursement depending on the number of advance tickets sold.

College and university bands rarely compete. In addition to the issues of time away from studies and the expense of traveling, the disparate styles (corps, Midwest high step, precision) would leave judges in a quandary.

Some parents are never fully apprised of judging criteria or exactly what sort of contest their children are involved in. There are independent contests which may be judged by people in the stadium pressbox. If a marching band circuit is involved, judges may be on the field. Circuit judging usually involves number scores. Independent competitions rank with word scores like "Good," "Excellent," "Superior," or "Outstanding." Directors will invariably receive in-depth analyses via audiocassettes the judges have utilized while observing the performance.

Spring/Summer Competitions

Some spring competitions involve parades only while others consist of parades, field shows, jazz band, orchestra, indoor guard and twirling.

219 All American Festivals
   1130 West Center Street
   North Salt Lake UT 84054

America's Youth on Parade *see*
   National Baton Twirling Association

220 Association of Scottish Games
   and Festivals
   5010 Mayfield Road, #206
   Lyndhurst OH 44124

221 Blossom Festival
   Niagara Falls, Ontario Canada

222 Cavalcade of Bands—Kentucky Derby Pegasus Parade
Kentucky Derby Festival Committee
137 W. Muhammed Ali Blvd.
Louisville KY 40202

223 Dakota Days Band Festival and Patriotic Parade
Box 747
Rapid City SD

224 Daytona Beach Music Festival
Daytona FL 32015

225 De Soto Band Contest
c/o The Spanish Manor House
910 Third Avenue West
Bradenton FL 34205

226 Dixie Classic Festivals
4964 Warwick Road
Richmond VA 23224
Sites: Richmond VA, Virginia Beach VA, Washington DC

227 Dogwood Arts Festival
Department of Parks and Recreation
P.O. Box 1631
Knoxville TN 37917

228 Festival
1701 East Parham Road, Suite 203
Richmond VA 23228

229 Festival of the States
c/o Suncoasters
1 Beach Drive S.E.
St. Petersburg FL 33731

230 Festivals of Music
Box 4A, Rt. 1
1784 W. Schuylkill Road
Douglassville PA 19518
Sites: Boston MA, Montreal, Canada; Myrtle Beach SC, Ocean City MD, San Antonio TX, Toronto, Canada; Virginia Beach VA, Washington DC, Williamsburg VA

231 Fiesta-Val Invitational Festivals for Band, Orchestra & Chorus
Spectrum of Richmond, Inc.
6219 Lakeside Avenue
Richmond VA 23228

232 Gateway Festivals
P.O. Box 1165
Monticello MN 55362
Many North American sites, including Atlanta, Orlando, Mexico City, Myrtle Beach, Rapid City, Toronto, and Vancouver plus bowl game performances (Holiday, Hall of Fame, Peach) and cruises

233 Great Lakes Band Championships
Kenosha Band Boosters, Inc.
c/o Larry Simons
3600 52nd Street
Kenosha WI 53144

234 Heritage Festivals
P.O. Box 571187
302 West 5400 South, Suite 108
Salt Lake City UT 84156-1187
Sites: 25 North American cities including the Opryland Classic, Nashville TN, Williamsburg/Virginia Beach VA, Washington DC (Cherry Blossom Festival), Niagara Falls, Canada; Vancouver, Canada (Hyack Parade)

235 Homestead Productions Band Festivals
P.O. Box 304
Hummelstown PA 17036

Opposite: *Downington High School Blue and Gold Marching Band, Pennsylvania.*

Sites: "The Original" Chocolatetown (Hershey PA), Fun & Sun (Clearwater FL), Seaport (Gorton/Mystic CT), International Azalea (Norfolk VA)

236 Illinois Valley Marching Band Contest
Hall High School
800 West Erie Street
Spring Valley IL 61362

237 International Band Festival
Red River Exhibition Association
876 St. James Street
Winnipeg, Manitoba R3G 3J7
Canada

238 International Music Festivals
P.O. Box 41
Parchment MI 49004

239 Invitational Music Festivals
6219 Lakeside Avenue
Richmond VA 23228
Sites: Atlanta GA, Lakeland/ Orlando FL, Myrtle Beach SC, Nashville TN, Pigeon Forge/Gatlinburg TN, Richmond VA, Toronto, Canada; Virginia Beach VA, Washington DC, Williamsburg VA

240 Music in the Parks
Box 4A, Rt. 1
Douglassville PA 19518
Sites include Adventureland IA, Kings Dominion VA, Dorney Park PA, Six Flags Over Texas TX, Valleyfair MN, Opryland TN, Fiesta Texas TX

241 Music Maestro Please, Inc.
2006 Swede Road
Norristown PA 19401
Sites include Colorado Springs CO, Toronto, Canada; Rome, Italy; Philadelphia PA, Chicago IL

242 Music Showcase Festivals
P.O. Box 142
Boyertown PA 19512
Sites include Hersheypark PA, Kings Dominion VA, Cedar Point OH, Six Flags St. Louis MO, Frontier City OK, Magic Mountain CA, Lagoon & Pioneer Village UT

National Association of Music Festivals *see* Gateway Festivals and Performing Arts Consultants Music Festivals

243 National Baton Twirling Association
Box 266
Janesville WI 53545

244 National Cherry Blossom Festival
c/o DC Convention and Visitors Association
1575 I Street, N.W., Suite 250
Washington DC 20005

245 National Cherry Festival
P.O. Box 141
108 W. Grandview Parkway
Traverse City MI 49685

246 National Events
2964 West 4700 South, Suite 200
Salt Lake City UT 84118
Includes Peach Bowl, Hall of Fame Bowl, Holiday Bowl; cruises; Mexico City, Toronto, Canada; New York

247 North American Music Festivals
P.O. Box 36
50 Brookwood Drive, Suite 1
Carlisle PA 17013

248 Oahu Music Festival (Hawaii)
1033 Shive Lane
Bowling Green KY 42103

W.T. Chipman Junior School Marching Band, Harrington, Delaware.

249 Performing Arts Consultants
Music Festivals
P.O. Box 310
46 Chatham Road
Short Hills NJ 07078
   Many North American sites
   plus bowl game festivals

Prestige Festivals *see* "World of
Music" Festivals

250 St. Louis Gateway Music Festival
c/o Discover St. Louis Tours
7603 Forsyth Blvd.
St. Louis MO 63105

251 Shenandoah Apple Blossom
Festival
5 N. Cameron Street
Winchester VA 22601

252 Six Flags Festivals
c/o Educational Tour Consultants, Inc.
934 Baker Lane, Suite A
Winchester VA 22603

253 Smoky Mountain Music Festival
c/o Dr. W.J. Julian
601 Westborough Road
Knoxville TN 37909
   Site: Gatlinburg TN

254 Tournament Music Festivals,
Inc.
703 Robert Street
Mechanicsburg PA 17055
   Sites: Wildwood NJ, Wil-
   liamsburg VA, Hershey PA

255 Tulip Festival
Chamber of Commerce

P.O. Box 36
Orange City IA 51041
   Includes parades with street
   competitions

256 Tulip Time Festival
Holland Convention & Visitors
Bureau
171 Lincoln Avenue
Holland MI 49423
   Includes pre-parade street
   shows by four selected "Pre-
   miere Performance Bands"

257 Virginia Beach Music Festivals
Virginia Beach Division
Hampton Roads Chamber
of Commerce
4512 Virginia Beach Boulevard
Virginia Beach VA 23462-3099

Visions in Sound *see* Gateway Festivals

258 West Virginia Strawberry Festival
West Virginia Strawberry Festival Association
Buckhannon WV 26201

259 WMC (World Music Contest)
Foundation Kerkrade
P.O. Box 133
6460 AC Kerkrade
The Netherlands

260 "World of Music" Festivals
P.O. Box 178126
San Diego CA 92177
   Sites include Opryland, Nash-
   ville TN; DisneyLand; Sea
   World, San Diego CA; Hono-
   lulu HI

Fall/Winter Competitions

261 A.A. Stagg Marching Band
Jamboree
A.A. Stagg High School
Palos Hills IL 60465

262 Appalachian Marching Band
Festival
c/o Phi Mu Alpha Sinfonia
School of Music
Appalachian State University
Boone NC 28608

263 Arizona State Marching Band
Festival
c/o Arizona Music Educators
Association and Arizona
Band and Orchestra Direc-
tors Association
Dobson High School
1501 W. Guadelupe Road
Mesa AZ 85202

264 Arizona State University Band
Day
School of Music
Arizona State University
Tempe AZ 85287-0405

265 Arvin High School Contest
Arvin High School
Bakersfield CA 93203

266 Athens Invitational Marching
Festival
Athens High School Band
Boosters
Athens OH 45701

267 Atlantic States Marching Fes-
tival
Catamount Band Club, Inc.
Dalton GA 30720

268 Bakersfield Contest
Bakersfield College
1801 Panorama Drive
Bakersfield CA 93305-1299

269 Bald Eagle-Nittany
Ben Avenue
Mill Hall PA 17751

270 Band-O-Rama
Marietta Tourist and Con-
vention Bureau and Noon
Lions Club
Marietta OH 45750

271 Bay State High School March-
ing Band Competition
New England Scholastic Band
Association
17 Elizabeth Street
North Dartmouth MA 02747

272 Bermuda Invitational Marching Band Competition
Bermuda Dept. of Tourism
310 Madison Avenue, 2nd Floor
New York NY 10021

273 Billerica Invitational Marching
Band Competition
River Street
Billerica MA 01821

274 Bonanza of Bands Marching
Competition
Zanesville High School
Zanesville OH 43701

275 Bowl Games of America
c/o Heritage Festivals
P.O. Box 571187
302 W. 5400 South, Suite 108
Salt Lake City UT 84157-1187
Sites: Ft. Lauderdale FL
(Blockbuster), Tucson AZ
(Copper), Jacksonville FL
(Gator), Shreveport LA (In-
dependence), El Paso TX
(John Hancock), Meadow-
lands NJ (Kickoff Classic),
Memphis TN (Liberty), New
Orleans LA (Sugar), Las Ve-
gas Bowl

276 Boyertown Cavalcade of
Bands
Boyertown High School
Boyertown PA 19512

277 Cadets Marching Band Coop-
erative (NJ, NY, PA, VA)
New Jersey sites: Montclair,
Piscataway H.S., Morris Hills
H.S., Union H.S., Sayerville
H.S., Franklin H.S., Ridge-
wood H.S., North Warren
H.S., Pompton Lakes H.S.,
North Rockland H.S., Mount
Olive H.S., Moris Knolls
H.S., Westfield H.S., Hunter-
don Central H.S., Bergenfield
H.S., Governor Livingston
H.S., Verona H.S., Boonton
H.S., Pequannock H.S. New
York sites: Copiague H.S.,
Brentwood H.S., Monsignor
Farrell H.S., Division Avenue
H.S., Hofstra, Hicksville
H.S., Mahopac H.S., Sachem
H.S., Huntington H.S. Penn-
sylvania sites: Northwestern
Lehigh H.S., Nazareth H.S.,
Shamokin H.S., Mid-Valley
H.S., Stroudsburg H.S.;
Lackawanna County Stadium,
Scranton; West Perry H.S.;
West Chester University,
West Chester, PA. Cham-
pionships held at Giants Sta-
dium, East Rutherford, NJ

278 Carrollton Band Day
Carrollton R-7 School District
300 East 9th Street
Carrollton MO 64633

279 Cary Band Day
Cary High School Band
638 Walnut Street
Cary NC 27511

280 Cavalcade of Bands
Western Michigan University
Kalamazoo MI 49001

281 Cavalcade of Bands Associa-
tion (NJ, PA)
High school members include:
Archbishop Ryan (Philadel-
phia PA), Downingtown
(PA), Hatboro-Horsham
(Horsham PA), Manheim
Township (PA), North Penn
(Lansdale PA), Shikellamy
(Sunbury PA), Upper Darby
(PA), Upper Moreland (Wil-
low Grove PA), Wilson (West
Lawn PA). One of the com-
petitions is held at West Ches-
ter University. Championships
are held at Hershey PA

282 Cecil County Parade of Bands
(TOB)
Elkton High School
Elkton MD 21921

283 Clarkston Invitational
Clarkston High School
6595 Middle Lake Road
Clarkston MI 48346

Clovis Field Tournament *see* Western Scholastic Marching Band
Conference

284 Danville Invitational Band
Contest
Danville High School
E. Lexington Avenue
Danville KY 40422

285 D.C. Everest High School
Competition
D.C. Everest High School
Schofield WI 54476

286 Del Oro Golden Eagle Marching Band Spectacular (in-
cludes parade)
Del Oro High School
3301 Taylor Road
Loomis CA 95650

287 Devil's Mountain Invitational
P.O. Box 21516
Concord CA 94521

Opposite: *Cumberland Regional High School Indoor Guard, Seabrook, NJ.*

Sponsored by Blue Devils
Drum & Bugle Corps, Clayton Valey and Mt. Diablo
High School Marching Bands

288 Drums by the Sea
New England Scholastic Band Association
c/o Don Vasconcelles, President
17 Elizabeth St.
North Dartmouth MA 02747
Site: Hull MA

289 East Georgia Marching Band Festival and Championships
Statesboro High School
10 Lester Road
Statesboro GA 30458

290 Emerald Coast Marching Band Festival
c/o Randy Nelson, Director of Bands
Choctawhatchee High School
110 Racetrack Road
Ft. Walton Beach FL 32548

291 Emerald Regime Invitational
Live Oak High School
1505 E. Main St.
Morgan Hill CA 95037

292 Fall Fest Music Show
Franklin Park Park District
9560 Franklin Avenue
Franklin Park IL 60131

293 Festival of Bands
School of Music
University of Oregon
Eugene OR 97403
Site: Autzen Stadium

294 Festival of Champions
Department of Music
Murray State University
1 Murray Street
Murray KY 42071-3303

295 Festival of Champions Invitational Marching Competition

Lexington Music Boosters
103 Clever Lane
Lexington OH 44904

296 Florida Citrus Sports Holiday Music Festival
5850 Lakehurst Drive, Suite 205
Orlando FL 32819
(800) 932-6440

297 Franklin-Simpson Invitational Marching Contest
Franklin-Simpson High School
P.O. Box 339
Franklin KY 42134

298 Gilroy High School Field Show
Gilroy High School
Gilroy CA 95020

299 Glendale Field Tournament
Glendale Community College
6000 W. Olive Avenue
Glendale AZ 85302-3090

300 Gold Coast Marching Band Festival
Plantation High School
Fort Lauderdale Fl 33310
Includes parade

301 Golden Invitational Marching Band Festival
c/o Band of Gold
Largo High School
410 Missouri Avenue
Largo FL 34640

302 Golden State Tournament of Bands Championship
Clovis High School
Clovis CA 93612

303 Gulf Coast Marching Band Festival
Gulfport High School
Gulfport MS 39501

304 Hoover High School Field Show

Upper Darby (PA) High School Indoor Guard.

Hoover High School
Fresno CA 93706

305 Huron College Pow Wow
   Days

Huron College Music Depart-
   ment
Huron College
Huron SD 57350

306 Idaho Third District High
School Marching Band Festival
Boise State University
Music Department
1910 University Drive
Boise ID 83725-1560

307 Illini Marching Band Festival
Continuing Education and
Public Service in Music
University of Illinois
1005 West Nevada Street
Urbana IL 61801-3883
> Site: Zuppke Field, Memorial
> Stadium, University of Illinois, Champaign-Urbana

308 Independence High School Invitational
Independence High School
San Jose CA 95113

309 Indiana Tournament of Bands
Chesterton High School
651 W. Morgan Avenue
Chesterton IN 46304

310 Iowa High School State
Marching Band Contests
c/o Everett D. Johnson
Iowa High School Music Association
1605 S. Story Street
P.O. Box 10
Boone IA 50036
> Iowa sites: Cedar Rapids,
> Council Bluffs, Des Moines,
> Fort Dodge, Muscatine, Sheldon

311 James Logan High School
Field Show
James Logan High School
Union City CA 94587

312 James Madison University
Marching Band Contest
Music Department

James Madison University
Harrisonburg VA 22801

313 Kappa Kappa Psi Marching
Contest
Arkansas State University
Jonesboro AR 72401

314 Land O' Sky Marching Band
Festival
Enka Band Boosters
Enka High School
Enka NC 28728

315 Lawton Open Marching Contest
Eisenhower High School
52 & Gore Blvd.
Lawton OK 73505

316 Los Altos High School Field
Show Tournament
c/o Southern California
School Band and Orchestra
Association
P.O. Box 4706
Anaheim CA 92803-4706

317 Louisiana Tech Invitational
Marching Band Classic
Louisiana Tech University
Bands
P.O. Box 8608
Ruston LA 71272

318 Manteca High School Field
Show
Manteca High School
Manteca CA 95336

319 Marple-Newtown Band-A-
Rama (TOB)
Marple-Newtown High School
Newtown Square PA 19073

320 Merrill High School Competition
Merrill Senior High School
Merrill WI 54452
> Site: Jay Stadium

321 Mid-South Invitational
   Director of Bands
   Memphis State University
   Memphis TN 38152
      Site: Halle Stadium, Memphis

322 Mid-South Marching Band
   Competition
   Gadsden High School
   Gadsden AL 35092

323 Mid-South Marching Band
   Contest
   Austin Peay State University
   601 College Street
   Clarksville TN 37040

324 Midwest Ohio Marching Band
   Competition
   Marion Local High School
   Band
   1901 State Route 716
   Maria Stein OH 45860

325 Milan Invitational Marching
   Festival
   Milan High School
   Milan TN 38358

326 Mission Viejo Field Tourna-
   ments
   Mission Viejo High School
   25025 Chrisanta
   Mission Viejo CA 92691
      Two each season

327 Mississippi Invitational March-
   ing Band Festival
   Tupelo High School
   Tupelo MS 38801

328 Modesto High School Field
   Show
   Modesto High School
   Modesto CA 95350

329 Mount Vernon Invitational
   Marching Band Classic
   8515 Old Mount Vernon Road
   Alexandria VA 22309

330 New Castle County Field Band
   Festival
   Newark High School
   Newark DE 19711

331 New Mexico Tournament of
   Bands
   New Mexico State University
   Las Cruces NM 88001

332 New York State Field Band
   Conference
      High school sites: Jamestown,
      Cortland, Cicero-North Syra-
      cuse, Oswego, Medina, Nor-
      wich, Baldwinsville, West
      Genesee, Southwestern, Vic-
      tor, Liverpool, Orchard Park,
      Webster, New Hartord, East
      Syracuse Minoa, Jordan-El-
      bridge, Mohonasen, Falconer,
      Mahopac

333 Newark Marching Band Invitational
   Newark High School
   314 Granville
   Newark OH 43055

334 North Penn Knight of Sound
   (CBA)
   North Penn High School
   Lansdale PA 19446

335 Northeast Florida Marching
   Band Festival
   Nathan Bedford Forrest Senior
   High School
   5530 Firestone Road
   Jacksonville FL 32244-1599

336 Northeast Missouri State
   Marching Contest
   Northeast Missouri State Uni-
   versity
   Kirksville MO 63501

337 Northern Arizona University
   Marching Band Festival
   c/o Administrative Assistant

Hatboro-Horsham High School Indoor Guard, Horsham PA.

Northern Arizona University
Bands
Northern Arizona University
Flagstaff AZ 86001

338 Northern Kentucky Marching
Festival
c/o Dr. Ted Williams
Band Director
Campbell County High School
8000 Alexandria Pike
Alexandria KY 41001

339 Oak Grove High School Invi-
tational
Oak Grove High School
San Jose CA 95129

340 Pacific Coast Invitational
Marching Band Champion-
ships
c/o Karl Raschkes
Music/Drama Coordinator
Curriculum Planning and Co-
ordination
2575 Commercial Street S.E.
Salem OR 97302
Site: Sprague H.S., Salem OR

341 Pacific Grove Marching Band
Festival
Pacific Grove High School
615 Sunset Drive
Pacific Grove CA 93950

342 Payson Field Tournament
Payson High School
Payson UT 84651

343 Peach State Marching Festival
c/o Director of Bands
Rome High School
Rome GA 30161

344 Penncrest Marching Band
Classic (TOB)
Penncrest High School
134 Barren Road
Media PA 19063

345 Rocky Mountain Band Com-
petition
University Bands
Department of Music
Brigham Young University
C-550 HFAC
P.O. Box 26410
Provo UT 84602-6410

346 Somerset Musictown Festival
Somerset High School
Somerset MA 02722
Includes non-competitive pa-
rade and field show

347 South Carolina State Fair
Marching Band Festival
c/o Philip C. McIntyre
South Carolina Band Direc-
tor's Association
James F. Byrnes High School
P.O. Box 187, Highway 290
Duncan SC 29334

348 Southland Band Classic
Enterprise High School
500 Watts Avenue
Enterprise AL 36330

349 Spartan Marching Percussion
Festival
Band Parents Organization
Glenbrook North High School
2300 Shermer Road
Northbrook IL 60062
Includes college and high
school units

350 State of Illinois High School
Marching Band Champion-
ship
Music Department
Illinois State University
Normal IL 61761

351 Superchief Marching Festival
(CMBC)
Piscataway High School
Piscataway NJ 08854

352 Texas Tech Marching Festival
Kappa Kappa Psi & Tau Beta
Sigma
Texas Tech University
Lubbock TX 79408
    Mainly west Texas area high
    schools

353 Tipp City Mum Festival
Tipp City Mum Festival Committee
c/o Mr. Kelly Gillis
546 Michael's Place
Tipp City OH 45371

354 Tournament of Bands Association (NC, NJ, PA, DE,
MD, NY, OH)
    Sites include: Wilmington
    DE, Elkton MD, Folsom PA,
    Media PA, Norristown PA.
    Championships held at Lack-
    awanna County Stadium PA.
    High school members include,
    from Delaware: Brandywine,
    Caravel Academy, Caesar
    Rodney, Christiana, Concord,
    Lake Forest, Laurel, McKean,
    Salesianum, William Penn;
    from Maryland: Arundel,
    Chopticon, Colonel Richard-
    son, Elkton, North East,
    Northern Maryland, Queen
    Anne County, Rising Sun,
    South Carroll, Westminster;
    from New Jersey: Audubon,
    Clearview, Delsea, Deptford,
    Eastern Regional, Edgewood,
    Egg Harbor, Florence, Glou-
    cester City, Governor Liv-
    ingston, Haddon Heights,
    Hammonton, Holy Cross,
    Kingsway, Northern Garrett,
    Penns Grove, Pleasantville,
    Shawnee, Sterling, Toms
    River East, Triton, Washing-
    ton Township; from Ohio:
    Wadsworth; from Pennsyl-
    vania: Bellefonte, Bensalem,
    Bermudian Springs, Berwick,
    Bloomsburg, Carlisle, Cata-
    saqua, Cedar Crest, Central

Bucks West, Cocalico, Cum-
berland Valley, Delone Cath-
olic, East Pennsboro, Em-
maus, Governor Mifflin,
Hanover, Hazleton, Hender-
son, Lebanon, Lebanon
Catholic, Lock Haven, Me-
chanicsburg, Montrose,
Northern Lebanon, Northern
York, Penncrest, Pocono
Mountain, Redland, Ridley,
Shamokin, Sun Valley, Wil-
liamsport, Wyoming Area;
from Virginia: Kempsville,
Louisburg, Princess Anne,
Salem; from West Virginia:
Hedgesville, Jefferson, Key-
ser.

355 Tri-State Band Festival
c/o Luverne Area Chamber of
Commerce
102 East Main
Luverne MN 56156
    Includes Minnesota, Iowa,
    South Dakota

356 University of Arizona Band
Day
University of Arizona Bands
School of Music
Room 109
Tucson AZ 85721

357 University of Colorado Band
Day Festival
University Bands
Campus Box 302
University of Colorado
Boulder CO 80309-0302

358 University of Connecticut
Band Day
University of Connecticut
Marching Band
Dr. David L. Mills, Director
U-12, Department of Music
University of Connecticut
Storrs CT 06269-1012

Downingtown (PA) High School Drum Line.

359 Upper Darby Marching Band
Festival (CBA)
Upper Darby High School
Lansdowne Avenue
Upper Darby PA 19083

360 Virginia State Marching Band
Festival
c/o Virginia Music Educators
Association and Virginia
Band and Orchestra Direc-
tors Association
West Site
c/o Donald Williams
Christiansburg High School
Bands
100 Independence Blvd.
Christiansburg VA 24073
East Site
c/o Steve King
2844 Embassy Circle, N.W.
Roanoke VA 24019

361 Watsonville High School Invi-
tational Field Show
Watsonville High School
Watsonville CA 95076

362 Waunakee Fall Invitational
Waunakee High School
Waunakee WI 53597

363 West Central Illinois Field
Show Competition
c/o West Central Illinois
Marching Band Association
Jacksonville High School
Jacksonville IL 62650

West Chester University *see* Cadets Marching Band Cooperative,
Cavalcade of Bands Association

364 West Covina High School
Field Tournament
West Covina High School

1609 E. Camero Avenue
West Covina CA 91791

365 Western Illinois University
Marching Band Competition
Western Illinois University
Macomb IL 61455

366 Western Scholastic Marching
Band Conference
c/o Allan Kristensen
Clovis High School
1055 N. Fowler Avenue
Clovis CA 93710
8 contests

367 Western States High School
Band Competition
University of Utah
Salt Lake City UT 84112

368 Westminster Field Tournament
Westminster High School
Westminster CA 92683

369 Wetumka Marching Competi-
tion
Wetumka High School
P.O. Box 8
Wetumka OK 74883

370 Wilson Sound Panorama
(CBA)
Wilson High School
West Lawn PA 19609

371 Wisconsin State Marching
Band Festival
c/o Waunakee High School
Waunakee WI 53597
1993 site: Camp Randall Stadium, University of Wisconsin–Madison

372 Wyoming State High School
Marching Band Champion-
ship
Casper WY 82601

Opposite: *Salesianum High School Marching Band, Wilmington DE.*

Associations

373 All American Association of
Contest Judges
1627 Lay Blvd.
Kalamazoo MI 49001

374 Cadets Marching Band Cooperative
78 Central Avenue
P.O. Box 8
Hackensack NJ 07602-0008
(201) 487-5797
Sponsored by Cadets of Bergen County Drum Corps

375 Cavalcade of Bands Associa-
tion
c/o Mr. Carey Crumling
RD #6
Nancy Street
Hanover PA 17331

376 Marching Band Association of
Southern California
200 Main Street, Suite 104-401
Huntington Beach CA 92648

377 Mid-Atlantic Judges Association
c/o Jim Althouse, Chief Judge
816 Center Avenue
Ephrata PA 17522

378 National Judges Association
c/o William Wildemore
134 Germantown Avenue
Plymouth Meeting PA 19462

379 New England Scholastic Band
Association
c/o Don Vasconcelles, President
17 Elizabeth Street
North Dartmouth MA 02747
Or: Joe Nee, Coordinator
417 Elk Run
Hudson NH 03051

380 New York Field Band Conference
c/o Rick Eleck
Cortland High School
Cortland NY 13045

381 Ohio Music Educators Association
Affiliated with Music Educators National Conference
1902 Association Drive
Reston VA 22091

382 Pennsylvania Federation of
Contest Judges
c/o Lee Kumer
2009 Luehm Avenue
North Versailles PA 15137-2601

383 South Carolina Band Direc-
tor's Association
c/o Philip C. McIntyre
Marching Committee Chair
James F. Byrnes High School
P.O. Box 187, Highway 290
Duncan SC 29334

384 Southern California School
Band and Orchestra Asso-
ciation
P.O. Box 4706
Anaheim CA 92803-4706
Provides judges for field
shows and parades sponsored
by other organizations

385 Texas Music Educators Association
c/o William Wildemore, Business Manager
134 Germantown Avenue
Plymouth Meeting PA 19462
Note: Addresses may change
as new presidents and chief
judges are elected.

Pennridge High School Twirlers, Perkasie P.A.

Selected Bibliography

Articles

387 Ake, H. Worth. "Consistency — A Much Used Word with Many Meanings for Judges, Instructors and Competitors." *Drum Corps News* (June 16, 1982): 8.

388 Brown, Elene C. "Music in Motion: 1992 Band Cavalcade Showcased." *Daily Local News* [West Chester PA] (October 15, 1992): F2.

389 Casavant, Albert R. "The Adjudication Process." *Instrumentalist* (August 1979): 23–24.

390 Dunnigan, Patrick. "Adapting to New Hash Marks." *Instrumentalist* (July 1993): 96.

391 Foster, Robert E. "Some Suggestions from a Marching Band Adjudicator." *School Musician, Director & Teacher* (August/September 1979): 10, 61–62.

392 Greenstone, Paul. "Philosophy of School Marching Bands." *School Musician, Director & Teacher* (October 1983): 10.

393 Guegold, William. "Substance, Not Style." *Instrumentalist* (January 1992): 80.

394 Hindsley, Mark H. "Adjudication in Perspective." *School Musician, Director & Teacher* (March 1980): 20–21.

395 Hong, Sherman. "Adjudicating the Marching Percussion Section." *Instrumentalist* (October 1981): 86–89.

396 Kenney, Edward L. "Bands Face Field of Tough Competition." *Sunday News Journal* [Wilmington DE] (October 28, 1984): G1, G4.

397 Lambrecht, Richard, and Prentice, Barbara. "A Checklist for Marching Bands." *Instrumentalist* (September 1990): 44, 49, 50, 52, 54.

398 Lautzenheiser, Tim. "Adjudication: Who Is the Real Judge?" *Instrumentalist* (September 1982): 114, 116.

399 _____. "Marching Band Competitions: Friend or Foe?" *Instrumentalist* (August 1981): 64.

400 Lovel, Walter. "The Contest Controversy." *Instrumentalist* (October 1983): 116.

401 "Marching Band Madness." *Sunset* (October 1981): 100–101.

402 Miller, Robert F. "How to Pick a Marching Band Contest." *Instrumentalist* (July 1984): 20, 22.

403 Moeny, Eugene E. "The Unification of Adjudication for Marching Bands and Contests." *School Musician, Director and Teacher* (October 1966): 70-71, 7.

404 Moyer, Ray. "Perfection?" *Instrumentalist* (January 1983): 86-87.

405 Neidig, Kenneth. "Realism, Efficiency, and Contest Excellence." *Instrumentalist* (September 1983): 31.

406 Rawlings, Randall. "Ten Weeks to Go." *Instrumentalist* (July 1980): 25.

407 Reely, Robert. "Learning from Contest Comments." *Instrumentalist* (August 1993): 79.

408 Rockefeller, David R. "Rifles, Pom-Poms, Flags, and Music?" *Music Educators Journal* (December 1982): 31-32.

409 Rogers, George L. "What Do Students and Parents Really Think?" *Instrumentalist* (September 1983): 22-24.

410 Sochinsky, James R., and Burnsed, Vernon. "The Band Interest Survey." *Instrumentalist* (September 1983): 29-30.

411 Soltwedel, Judy. "The Director's View." *Instrumentalist* (September 1983): 24, 26.

412 Stansberry, John C. "Soft Corps (An Alternative to Hard Corps)." *Instrumentalist* (October 1979): 21-22.

413 "Student Musicians at Athletic Events: Half-Time Education?" *Music Educators Journal* (December 1978): 24-31.

414 Telesco, Joseph. "Marching Styles — The Words That Cause Debate." *Instrumentalist* (September 1984): 120.

415 Van Vorst, Charles E. "Corps Style Bands: The Best of Both Worlds." *Instrumentalist* (April 1983): 6-7.

Books and Monographs

416 Bennett, George T. *Field Routines for Marching Band Contests and Public Exhibitions.* Marching Maneuver Series, Vol. VI. Chicago IL: Gamble Hinged Music Company, 1938.

417 _____. *Grooming the Marching Band for High School Contests.*

Marching Maneuver Series, Vol. III. Chicago IL: Gamble Hinged Music Company, 1937.

418 _____. *Required and Special Maneuvers for High School Marching Band Contests.* Marching Maneuver Series, Vol. IV. Chicago IL: Gamble Hinged Music Company, 1937.

419 Bilik, Jerry H. *Gridiron Showmanship.* Ann Arbor MI: Jerry Bilik Music, 1974.

Opposite: *Governor Livingston High School Marching Band, Berkeley Heights NJ.*

Part 3
Drum & Bugle Corps

Drum corps, like marching bands, are a fairly well kept secret, but each summer many stadiums throughout the United States reverberate to the strains of brass and percussion as children, teens, adults, and grandfolks compete under the aegis of such organizations as Drum Corps International (DCI) and Drum Corps Associates (DCA). There are still some all-male (DCI members, Madison Scouts, Cavaliers) corps. Internationally, there is a growing corps movement in Europe, especially Britain, and in Japan.

Besides brass and percussion, a drum corps is composed of silk (flag) and rifle squads. Although there are no woodwinds, twirlers or pom-pon squads, it appears that non-brass instruments may be experimented with in the near future.

Drum Corps International is composed of "junior" corps. Members' ages range from 14 to 21. Maximum corps number is 128. There are also Division II and Division III corps that also have championships. Obviously some high school and college musicians need or want summer jobs, and some corps recognize this and concentrate their performances on weekends in a specific region; e.g., the Jersey Surf travels the northeast. The top 12 at the DCI 1993 World Championships held in Jackson, Mississippi, were: (1) Cadets of Bergen County, Hackensack NJ, (2) Star of Indiana, Bloomington IN, (3) Phantom Regiment, Rockford/Loves Park IL, (4) Blue Devils, Concord CA, (5) Cavaliers, Rosemont IL, (6) Madison Scouts, Madison WI, (7) Santa Clara Vanguard, Santa Clara CA, (8) Crossmen, Bensalem PA (9) Bluecoats, North Canton OH, (10) Blue Knights, Denver CO, (11) Glassmen, Toledo OH, (12) Colts, Dubuque IA. The top 25 corps comprise the voting membership of DCI. Many corps draw on several states for their members, and headquarters change. The Sky Ryders used to hale from Kansas. Now it's Texas. The Crossmen have moved around eastern Pennsylvania and often rehearse in New Jersey.

Drum Corps Associates was organized in 1965. There are no age restrictions on membership. As with DCI, a corps numbers 128. As of 1993 there were 20 DCA member corps, including the Buccaneers, Chieftains, Westshoremen, Musketeers, Thunderbirds, and Ambassadors from Pennsylvania; Matadors from Rhode Island; Hurricanes from Connecticut; Caballeros, Skyliners, Sunrisers, and Crusaders from New York; Bushwackers from New Jersey; and Regionaires from Canada. The 1993 championships were held in Scranton, Pa.

Competition schedules are found in DCI Today *and* Drum Corps World.

Associations

420 Drum Corps Associates
10 Columbus Drive
Monmouth Beach NJ 07750

421 Drum Corps East
c/o Tony DiCarlo
Executive Director
246 West Street
South Weymouth MA 02188

422 Drum Corps International
c/o Mary Pandolfo
Marketing and Development
P.O. Box 548
1263 S. Highland Avenue
Lombard IL 60148
> Future World Championships
> sites: 1994 – Boston MA;
> 1995 – Jacksonville FL; 1996 –
> Lansing MI; 1997 – Buffalo
> NY; 1998 – Jackson MS;
> 1999 – west of the Rockies;
> 2000 – Jacksonville FL.

423 Drum Corps Midwest
c/o Roman Blenski
Executive Director
4601 W. Holt Avenue
Milwaukee WI 53219

424 Drum Corps New York
c/o Carl Pyns
P.O. Box 22
Wampsville NY 13163

425 Drum Corps South
c/o Jim Meals
421 W. Spruce Street
Titusville PA 16372

426 Drum Corps United Kingdom
c/o J. Garton, Oliver Hind
Club
Edale Road
Sneiton Dale
Nottingham NG2 4HT
England

427 Drum Corps West
c/o Tom Hope
Executive Director
372 Florin Road, Suite 303
Sacramento CA 95831

428 F.A.M.Q.
c/o Carol Plante or Rachel
Ouimet
Box 1000 – Succursale M.
Montreal, Quebec
Canada H1V 3R2

429 Ontario Drum Corps Association
c/o Lyne Sosnowski
258 King Street North, Suite
12J
Waterloo, Ontario
Canada N2J 2Y9

Selected Bibliography

Articles

430 "Beating the Drums for the Corps." *Sports Illustrated* (August 10, 1987): 18.

Fleetwood (PA) High School Indoor Guard.

431 Cahill, Michael J. "A Capsule History of the Drum and Bugle Corps." *The Instrumentalist* (June 1982): 6–9.

432 Carter, Kevin L. "Hard Corps." [Crossmen] *Philadelphia Inquirer* (August 9, 1993): C5, C12.

433 Kachin, Denise Breslin. "Everything but 76 Trombones." *Philadelphia Inquirer* (June 6, 1991): 4-CC–5-CC plus cover photo.

434 Karis, Al. "A Little History: Notable Anniversaries in the Drum Corps Activity." *Drum Corps World* (April 1982): 10.

435 Koizumi, Katsuyuki. "Corps Questions." *The Instrumentalist* (October 1982): 8. "The Author Replies" by Michael Cahill.

436 McCarthy, Pat, and McCarthy, Paul. "The Art of Drum Corps Percussion—Some Comments About the Past, Present and Future Trends." *Drum Corps News* (January 27, 1982): 8–9.

437 McGrath, William A. "The Contribution of Senior Drum and Bugle Corps to Marching Percussion." *Percussionist* (Spring/Summer 1980): 149–176.

438 "Marching Band vs. Drum Corps: One Marching Member's Opinion." *Percussive Notes* (July 1983): 56–57.

440 "The 1983 Drum Corps Hit Parade, Management, Instructors, Historical Notes." *Drum Corps News* (July 8, 1983): 8–9, 13–15.

441 Orgill, Roxane. "No Strings: Summer with the Drum and Bugle Corps." *Wall Street Journal* (September 18, 1990): A18, A28.

442 Roznoy, Richard T. "The Drum Corps International Championships." *Instrumentalist* (June 1978): 24–27.

443 Spalding, Dan C. "The Evolution of Drum Corps Drumming." *Percussionist* (Spring/Summer 1980): 116–131.

444 "Sports Medicine Practiced in Regiment's Musical Sport." *DCI Today* (November-December 1992): 8–9.

445 Vickers, Steve. "Drum Corps Moves into the '80s." *Instrumentalist* (June 1980): 18–19.

446 _____. "The Drum Corps World in 1982." *Instrumentalist* (June 1982): 10–11.

447/448 _____. "1984 Report: Drum Corps World." *Instrumentalist* (June 1984): 9–11.

Books

449 Bennett, George T. *New and Novel Formations for Marching Bands and Drum Corps.* Marching Maneuver Series, Vol. VII. Chicago IL: Gamble Hinged Music Company, 1938.

450 Blake, Richard I. *The Music of the Hawthorne Caballeros.* Lynn MA: Fleetwood Records, 1961.

451 *Competitive Drum Corps, There and Then ... to Here and Now.* Des Plaines IL: Olympic Printing, 1981.

452 *The 1992 Summer Music Games.* Lombard IL: Drum Corps International. 1992. Souvenir championships program featuring 20-year history of DCI.

453 Petty, Mark A. *Corps Style Percussion Techniques.* Troy MI, 1976.

454 Popp, Jodeen E. *Competitive Drum Corps.* Des Plaines IL: Olympic Printing, 1979.

Part 4
Fund-Raising

General

The ways to raise money for a trip, instruments, or uniforms are limited only by one's imagination. Candy always sells but does not provide a high profit margin. Raffles can net plenty, but even turkey or ham raffles are illegal in some states. Records and cassettes made from concerts or field shows are novel but can be expensive. Cheap jewelry is virtually a one-time-only method. Other traditional ways to raise money are sausage and cheese, hoagies/submarines/sandwiches (preferably made on a school's in-service day so that lunchtime deliveries can be made to local businesses), spaghetti dinners, flowers, dance-a-thons, ceramic Christmas ornaments, candles, fruit, car washes, bingo, auctions, and selling refreshments at concerts, games, and competitions. Band performance videos are newer items.

One nontraditional method for raising funds that nets one hundred percent profit for the student or music fund is a band calendar. Use black and white photos, one per month, each featuring a different section of the band. The printing costs can be defrayed through local businesses that supply business cards for reproduction around each photo and pay, say, $25 per ad. Six ads per month equals $150, twelve months times $150 equals $1,800 and voilà, the printing cost is zero. Sell the calendar cheap, and sell a lot. Take the photos during band camp or early in the autumn season so the calendars can be printed and sold before Christmas.

To get a truck to transport equipment, try canvassing local businesses. In return for their money, the truck can advertise their products and services.

Fund-Raising Organizations and Products

Note: Yellow Pages in most cities' telephone directories include a fund-raising category.

455 Agents Card & Gift Company
4543 Third Avenue
Bronx NY 10458

456 Alamo Fruit
Alamo TX 78516

457 America's Best Chocolate, Inc.
116 Spencer Street
Brooklyn NY 11205

458 B-Craft Fund Raising Products
5801 65th Avenue, North
Minneapolis MN 55429

Kutztown (PA) High School Indoor Guard.

459 Best Citrus of Florida
P.O. Box 3333
Fort Pierce FL 33454

460 Buckeye Donkey Ball Company
P.O. Box 345
Marengo OH 43334

461 Christmas Ridge Handcrafts
Div. C.A.P., Inc.
322 Crab Orchard Road
Lancaster KY 40445
Wreaths

462 Crest Fruit Company
121 N. Tower Rd.
Alamo TX 78516

463 Cromer's P-Nuts, Inc.
1235 Assembly Street
P.O. Box 163
Columbia SC 29201

464 Drum Corps Midwest
4601 West Holt Ave.
Milwaukee WI 53219

465 Florida Indian River Groves
P.O. Box 698
Ft. Pierce FL 34954

466 The Foreign Candy Company
451 Black Forest Road
Hull IA 51239

467 Four Point Products
622 2nd Avenue
Pittsburgh PA 15219

468 Friendship House
29313 Clemens Road, #2-G
P.O. Box 450978
Cleveland OH 44145-0623

469 Fun Services Games & Supplies
500 Bennett
Elk Grove Village IL 60007

470 G & S Sales Company
37 N. Albany Avenue
Atlantic City NJ 08401

471 Genesis Productions, Inc.
7358 N. Lincoln Avenue
Lincolnwood
Chicago IL 60646

472 Georgia Music & Video
908 Willow Trail Drive
Norcross GA 30093

473 Gold Medal Products Company
2001 Dalton Avenue West End
Cincinnati OH

474 Hale Indian River Grove
P.O. Box 217
Wabasso FL 32970

475 Henco, Inc.
205 Henco Drive
Selmer TN 38375
Customized community game

476 Langdon Barber Groves
P.O. Box 1088
Vero Beach FL 32961

477 Manor Bakery
P.O. Box 19090
Little Rock AR 72219

478 MBM Enterprises
c/o Marilyn Machi
7228 Baptist Road, Suite 160
Bethel Park PA 15102

479 Mickman Bros. Nurseries
14630 Highway 65
Anoka MN 55304

480 National Fund Raising Consultants, Inc.
8341 S. Sangre De Cristo Road
Littleton CO 80127

481 Nestle-Beich Candies
Front & Lumber Streets
Bloomington IL 61701

482 Pennsylvania Dutch Funnel
   Cake Company
   P.O. Box 35
   Sewell NJ 08080

483 QSP/Quality School Plan
   P.O. Box 10203
   Des Moines IA 50306

484 Revere Company
   P.O. Box 119, Dept. H22
   Scranton PA 18504-0119

485 Riversweet Citrus
   11350 66th Street North, Suite
      102
   Largo FL 34643

486 Ross Galleries, Inc.
   761-D Coates Avenue
   Holbrook NY 11741
      Art auctions, ad books, raffles

487 School Fund Properties, Inc.
   43 E. Ohio Street
   Chicago IL 60611

488 Sherwood Forest Farms
   P.O. Box 789
   Chehalis WA 98532

489 Sunkist Fund Raising
   Sunkist Growers, Inc.
   P.O. Box 7888
   Van Nuys CA 91409

490 Sunsweet Fruit Corporation
   Box 3264 or Drawer T
   Vero Beach FL 32960

491 Tootsie Roll Industries, Inc.
   7401 S. Cicero Avenue
   Chicago IL 60629

492 Velva-Sheen Manufacturing
      Company
   3860 Virginia Avenue
   Cincinnati OH 45227

493 Wolfgang Homestead, Inc.
   P.O. Box 165
   York PA 17405
      Sweet Note Chocolate

494 Worth Distributing Company,
      Inc.
   490 Lancaster Avenue
   Frazer PA 19355

Selected Bibliography

Articles

495 Cornock, Ruth. "Fund-Raising Tips for Bands on the Move." *Instrumentalist* (October 1983): 58, 60–62.

496 Darnall, Josiah. "Fund-Raising Ideas Ripe for the Picking." *Instrumentalist* (April 1987): 27–28, 30.

497 Laich, Ralph. "You Don't Stumble Over Mountains." *School Musician, Director & Teacher* (December 1982): 6–9.

498 Tubbs, Ann Marie. "What a Way to Make a Buck." *Instrumentalist* (January 1982): 82.

Books

499 Arledge, Rick, and Friedman, David. *Dynamic Fund Raising Projects.* Chicago: Precept Press.

500 Brownrigg, W. Grant. *Effective Corporate Fundraising.* New York: American Council for the Arts.

501 Edles, L. Peter. *Fundraising: Hand-on Tactics for Nonprofit Groups.* New York: McGraw-Hill.

Part 5
Indoor Guard

Indoor guard, also known as indoor cavalcade or winter guard, is a gymnasium competition that takes place in winter and spring and involves junior and senior high school, college, and independent units. For some, indoor guard is an opportunity for the band front to maintain and hone skills during the off-season, but for others it is an exciting and challenging activity in its own right. High school associations, such as the Cavalcade Indoor Drill Association (CIDA), include baton twirling squads as well as color guards in their contests. In recent years drum lines have also competed in CIDA.

Color guards and twirlers perform intricate—and frequently dangerous—routines to prerecorded music: rock, opera, movie, Broadway. Dance training is evident in the balletic and jazz moves of many units. For extra traction, some units bring their own tarps that cover the gymnasium floor. Colorful backdrops frame the performers who use flags, rifles, and sabers as well as props deemed appropriate to the show: chimneys with fire extinguisher smoke, remote control flag shooters, plywood saloons and locomotives, full-scale gazebos, theater marquees, and paddlewheel steamships. Cheap props include rakes, children's hockey sticks, bar stools, folding chairs, and plastic milk boxes nailed to wood to create light platforms.

Associations

502 California Color Guard Circuit
c/o Ron Nankervis
201 S. 4th, #537
San Jose CA 95112-3659

503 Carolina Color Guard Circuit
c/o Michael Gray
175 Second Street
Cheraw SC 29520-2729

504 Cavalcade Indoor Drill Association (CIDA)
c/o Robert Everitt
441 Bridge Street
Graterford PA 18944

505 Cecq
c/o Ginette Ringuette
762 Boulevard
Samson Laval, Quebec
    H7X 1K1
Canada

506 Central Valley Guard Circuit
c/o Gary Runsten
641 Norseman Drive
Modesto CA 95351

507 Continental Divide Color Guard Circuit
c/o Kevin Moris

5306 South Broadway Circle,
#4-101
Englewood CO 80110-5734

508 CYO Color Guard Circuit
c/o Paul Cain
48 Irving Street
Everett MA 02149-4826

509 Eastern Massachusetts Color
Guard Circuit
c/o Harry Sampson
8 Highland Avenue
Stoneham MA 02180-1870

510 Florida Federation of Color
Guard
c/o Cheryl Wimberley
5791 North University Club
Boulevard #501
Jacksonville FL 32211

511 Gulf Coast Color Guard Circuit
c/o J.C. Connor
4561 Scarlet Drive
Crestview FL 32536-6302

512 Indiana Color Guard Circuit
c/o Bob and Ruth Ann Med-
worth
1 Knight Drive
Brazil IN 47834

513 Keystone Indoor Drill Association (KIDA, PA)
c/o Chuck Saia, Administrative Coordinator
1531 Vesta Drive
Harrisburgh PA 17112
Or: Phillip Hower
1411 Esther Drive
Lebanon PA 17042-9135

514 Metropolitan American Asso-
ciates/EMBA Color Guard
c/o Matthew Cornelisse
336 Standish Avenue
Hackensack NJ 07601

515 Michigan Color Guard Circuit
c/o Laura Good
9686 Winston
Redford MI 48239-1660

516 Midwest Color Guard Circuit
c/o Diane Miller
6N730 Hillside Court
Medinah IL 60157

517 Mid-York Color Guard Circuit
c/o Craig Elwood
2 Collins Terrace
Central Square NY 13036-9300

518 National Judges Association
c/o Dom Fulginiti
703 Roberts Street
Mechanisburg PA 17055

519 North Star Color Guard
Circuit
c/o M. Hankanen
P.O. Box 18474
St. Paul MN 55118-0474

520 Northeast Color Guard Circuit
c/o Dick Greene
112 Dyke Street
Wellsville NY 14895-1614

521 Northern California Winter
Guard Circuit
c/o Ron Nankervis
San Jose Raiders
1525 Almaden Road
San Jose CA 95125

522 Northwest Pageantry Association
c/o Nancy Beley
22602 115th Place S.E.
Kent WA 98031-2673

523 Ohio Color Guard Circuit
c/o Fred Miller
118 Westpark
Centerville OH 45459-4815

524 Oklahoma Color Guard
    Circuit
    c/o Larry Shockley
    4005 Stonebridge Circle
    Yukon OK 73099-3215

525 Ontario Color Guard Associa-
    tion
    c/o Lynne Sosnowski
    122 King Street South #201
    Waterloo, Ontario N2P 1P5
    Canada

526 Pennsylvania Federation of
    Contest Judges
    c/o Lee Kumer
    2009 Luehm Avenue
    North Versailles PA 15137-2601

527 San Joaquin Color Guard As-
    sociation
    c/o Bruce Morow/Clovis
    School District
    1450 Herndon Avenue
    Clovis CA 93611-0567

528 South Florida Color Guard
    Circuit

529 Southeast Color Guard Circuit
    c/o Alan Hunt
    415 8th Street N.W.
    Cleveland TN 37311-1870

530 Southern California Color
    Guard Association
    c/o Noreen Roberts
    16401 Golden Gate
    Huntingdon Beach CA 92649
        Or: Lee Carlson
        31-120 Avenida El Mundo
        Cathedral City CA 92234

c/o Tony Florio
1507 Argyle Drive, #208
Fort Lauderdale FL 33312-1576

531 Texas Color Guard Associa-
    tion
    c/o Danny Gatlin
    P.O. Box 23
    Alvord TX 76225-0023

532 Tournament of Bands Indoor
    Drill Association (TIDA)
    c/o William Wildemore, Busi-
    ness Manager
    134 Germantown Avenue
    Plymouth Meeting PA 19462

533 VFW
    c/o Bob Brady, Chairman
    National Marching Units and
    Parade Committee
    319 Tadmore Road
    Ross Township
    Perryville PA 15237

534 Virginia Area Color Guard
    Circuit
    c/o Anne Coldiron
    1602 Bexhill Road
    Richmond VA 23229-4707

535 West Penn Color Guard Cir-
    cuit
    c/o James Kraus
    125 Parkfield Street
    Pittsburgh PA 15210

536 Winter Guard International
    c/o Ms. Lynn Lindstrom
    6834 Balsam Street
    Arvada CO 80004

Band Front and Color Guard Equipment

537 Acme Canvas Co. Inc.
    171 Medford Street

Malden MA 02148
Floor covers

Newark High School Yellowjacket Marching Band, Newark, Delaware.

538 Band Mans Company
10660 Wireway, Suite 201
Dallas TX 75220

539 Bernie Roe & Associates
P.O. Box 4525
Ithaca NY 14852
   Includes batons, flags,
   rifles, t-shirts, buttons

540 Fred J. Miller Inc.
118 West Park Road
Dayton OH 45459

541 George Miller & Sons
209 E. Church Street
Blackwood NJ 08012

542 Intermedia, Inc.
85 Carver Avenue
Westwood NJ 07675

543 SEFCO Plumes
Division, Kerr's Music World
911 Bigley Avenue
Charleston WV 25302

544 Tom Peacock's Maces and Batons
956-D South Anaheim Blvd.
Anaheim CA 92805

545 WMWG Inc.
442½ Bridge Street NW
Grand Rapids MI 49504
   Forte sabers

Selected Bibliography

Articles

546 Biondi, Christopher, and Kennedy, Tom. "Pizza, Hoagies Rushed to Stranded Students." *Daily Local News* [West Chester PA] (March 14, 1993): A1, A4.

547 Burns, Caroline. "Field of View Likes Competing." *Daily Local News* [West Chester PA] (April 12, 1993): A5. Includes two photos.

548 Fuller, John. "The Flag Corps." *School Musician, Director & Teacher* (June/July 1979): 36–39, 46.

549 Holston, Kim. "They Call It Indoor Guard." *Twirl* (June/July/August 1980): 16.

550 Kachin, Denise Breslin. "Amid All That White, a Parade of Color." *Philadelphia Inquirer* (March 21, 1993): CC6.

551 Kennedy, Tom. "WCU Color Guard Team Shines in International Show." *Daily Local News* [West Chester PA] (March 2, 1992): A1, B1. Includes three photos (Tsunami Blue, Phoenix, Field of View).

552 Masoner, Betty L. "The Guard—With Color." *School Musician, Director & Teacher* (May 1981): 18–20.

553 Meagher, Marlene. "Effective Flags — A Basic Approach." *Instrumentalist* (March 1985): 38–40.

554 Pfeifle, Morell. "The Color Guard." *School Musician, Director & Teacher* (May 1978): 55, 59.

555 Sagen, Dwayne P. "Flags That Visualize Music." *Instrumentalist* (October 1977): 49–54.

Books

556 *Championship Auxiliary Units.* Sherman Oaks CA: Alfred Publishing Company, 1979.

Part 6
Military Bands

Directory

557 Admiral Farragut Academy
Pine Beach NJ 08741

558 Armed Forces School of Music
LFTC, Marine Element
Little Creek
Norfolk VA 23521-5240

559 Army and Navy Academy
Carlsbad CA 92008

560 Benedictine Military Institute
304 North Sheppard Street
Richmond VA 23221

561 Benedictine Military School
6502 Seawright Drive
Savannah GA 31406

562 Camden Military Academy
Camden SC 29020

563 Carson Long Institute Drum
and Bugle Corps
New Bloomfield PA 17068

564 The Citadel
Charleston SC 29409

565 Culver Military Academy
Culver IN 46511

566 Fishburne Military School
Waynesboro VA 22980

567 Florida Air Academy
1950 South Academy Drive
Melbourne FL 32901

568 Fork Union Military Academy
Fork Union VA 23055

569 Georgia Military College
Milledgeville GA 31060

570 Hargrave Military Academy
Chatham VA 24531

571 Howe Military School
Howe IN 46746

572 Kemper Military School/College
Boonville MO 65233

573 La Salle Military Academy
Drum and Bugle Corps
Oakdale, Long Island NY
11769

574 Lyman Ward Military Academy
Camp Hill AL 36850

575 Maine Maritime Academy
Castine ME 04421

576 Marine Corps Field Section
Headquarters, U.S. Marine
Corps
Washington DC 20380-0001

577 Marine Military Academy
Harligen TX 78550

578 Marion Military Institute
Marion AL 36756

579 Marmion Military Academy
Aurora IL 60504

580 Massachusetts Maritime Academy
Buzzards Bay MA 03532

581 Massanutten Military Academy
Drum and Bugle Corps
Woodstock VA 22664

582 Midshipman Drum and Bugle
Corps
U.S. Naval Academy
Annapolis MD 21402

583 Missouri Military Academy
Mexico MO 65262

584 New Mexico Military Institute
Roswell NM 88201

585 New York Military Academy
Cornwell-On-Hudson NY 12520

586 North Georgia College
Dahlonega GA 30533

587 Northwestern Military Academy Drum and Bugle Corps
Lake Shore Drive
Lake Geneva WI 53147

588 Norwich University
Northfield VT 05663

589 Oak Ridge Military Academy
Oak Ridge NC 27310

590 Randolph-Macon Academy
Front Royal VA 22630

591 Riverside Military Academy
Gainesville GA 30501

592 St. John's College/HS
2607 Military Drive
Washington DC 20015

593 St. John's Military Academy
Delafield WI 53018

594 St. John's Military School
Salina KS 67401

595 San Marcos Academy
San Marcos TX 78666

596 SUNY Maritime College
Fort Schuyler
Bronx NY 10465

597 Texas A&M University
College Station TX 77843

598 Texas Military Institute
20955 West Tejas Trail
San Antonio TX 78257-1604

599 U.S. Air Force Academy Band
USAF Academy
Colorado Springs CO 80840

600 U.S. Air Force Band
Superintendent
Building 422, Bolling Air Force Base
Washington DC 20332-6458

601 U.S. Army Band ("Pershing's Own")
Brucker Hall, Building 480
Fort Myer VA 22211-5050

602 U.S. Coast Guard Band
U.S. Coast Guard Academy
New London CT 06320

603 U.S. Marine Band
8th & I Streets, S.E.
Washington, DC 20390-5000

604 U.S. Merchant Marine Academy
Kings Point NY 11024

605 U.S. Military Academy Band
OIC Cadet Band
U.S. Military Academy
West Point NY 10996

606 U.S. Naval Academy Band
U.S. Naval Academy
101 Buchanan Road, Mail Stop 3A
Annapolis MD 21402-5080

607 U.S. Navy Band
Washington Navy Yard, Building 105-2
901 M Street, S.E.
Washington DC

608 Valley Forge Military Academy & Junior College

1001 Eagle Road
Wayne PA 19087-3695

609 Virginia Military Institute
Lexington VA 24450

610 Virginia Polytechnic Institute
Blacksburg VA 24061

611 Wentworth Military Academy
Lexington MO 64067

Associations

612 Company of Fifers and Drummers
P.O. Box 525
620 N. Main Street
Ivorytown CT 06442

613 Military School Band Associa-
tion
MAJ Ronald Horton
Newsletter
Fork Union Military Academy
Fork Union VA 23055

Selected Bibliography

Articles

614 Blair, Dennis K. "Music in the Military." *Instrumentalist* (November 1986): 54, 56.

615 Cochran, Alfred W. "Military Bands — An Aid to Music Education." *Instrumentalist* (August 1984): 10.

616 Maiello, Anthony J. "The Battle Over Military Bands." *Instrumentalist* (October 1992): 112.

617 "Merchant Marine Cadets Hear Beat of a Different Drummer." *Journal of Commerce* (November 14, 1991): 10A.

618 Modi, Sorab. "The United States Marine Band." *Ovation* (June 1989): 16–18, 80.

619 Outerbridge, Laura. "Strike Up the Bands: Military Music Tradition Marches On." *Washington Times Weekend* (May 28, 1992): M4, M5.

620 Richards, William W. "Percussion in the Military." *Percussive Notes* (October 1984): 31–32.

621 "The U.S. Military Academy Band, West Point." *Instrumentalist* (December 1981): 26–27.

North East High School Blue Crew Marching Band, North East, Maryland.

622 Young, Amanda. "Music in the Military." *Music Educators Journal* (December 1981): 31–35, 54–56.

Books and Dissertations

623 Adkins, H.E. *Treatise on the Military Band.* Rockville Centre NY: Belwin, 1945.

624 Carpenter, Kenneth William. *A History of the United States Marine Band.* [Ph.D. dissertation] Iowa City: University of Iowa, 1970. Excerpted in *ABA Journal of Band Research* (Spring 1971): 23–28.

625 Glasgow, William. *Exhibition Drills.* Harrisburg PA: Military Service Publishing Company, 1958.

626 Railsback, Thomas C., and Langellier, John P. *The Drums Would Roll: A Pictorial History of U.S. Army Bands on the American Frontier, 1866–1900.* New York: Sterling Publishing Company, 1988.

627 United States Department of the Army. *The Marching Band.* Washington DC, 1957.

Part 7
Musicians, Instruments and Uniforms

Associations

Academy of Wind and Percussion Arts *see* National Band Association

628 American Music Conference
5140 Avenida Encinas
Carlsbad CA 92008

629 American Musical Instrument Society
c/o The Shrine to Music Museum
414 E. Clark Street
Vermillion SD 57069

630 First Chair of America
c/o Mary Martin
P.O. Box 474
Greenwood MS 38930

631 International Clarinet Society
P.O. Box 7683
Shawnee Mission KS 66207-0683

632 International Horn Society
c/o Ellen Powley
2220 N. 1400 East
Provo UT 84604

633 International Trombone Association
c/o Vern Kagarice
North Texas State University
School of Music
Denton TX 76203

634 International Trumpet Guild
Florida State University
School of Music
Tallahassee FL 32306

635 Music Educators National Conference
1902 Association Drive
Reston VA 22091-1597

636 National Association of Band Instrument Manufacturers
38 West 21st Street
New York NY 10010-6906

637 National Association of College Wind and Percussion Instructors
Division of Fine Arts
Northeast Missouri State University
Kirksville MO 63501

638 National Association of Music Merchants
5140 Avenida Encinas
Carlsbad CA 92008-4391

639 National Association of Professional Band Instrument Repair Technicians
Box 51
Normal IL 61761-0051

640 National Association of Rudimental Drummers
Defunct

641 National Association of School Music Dealers
4020 McEwen, Suite 105
Dallas TX 75244-5019

642 National Association of Uniform Manufacturers and Distributors
1156 Avenue of the Americas, Suite 700
New York NY 10036
Sponsors Best Dressed Bands Awards Program

643 National Band Association
P.O. Box 121292
Nashville TN 37212

644 National Flute Association
c/o Myrna Brown

805 Laguna
Denton TX 76201

645 North American Saxophone
Alliance
c/o Dale Underwood
13408 Piscataway
Ft. Washington MD 20744

646 Percussive Arts Society
123 W. Main
Urbana IL 61801

647 Tubists Universal Brotherhood
Association
c/o Skip Gray
University of Kentucky
School of Music
Lexington KY 40506-0022

Music Fraternities and Sororities

648 Kappa Kappa Psi National
Honorary Band Fraternity
P.O. Box 849
Stillwater OK 74074

Modern Music Masters *see* Tri-M
Music Honor Society

649 Tri-M Music Honor Society
c/o Music Educators National

Conference
1902 Association Drive
Reston VA 22091-1597

650 Tau Beta Sigma National Honorary Band Sorority
P.O. Box 849
Stillwater OK 74074

Instrument Manufacturers and Distributors

The Yellow Pages of the telephone book will include local stores. Buy-sell newspapers are helpful for those seeking used instruments.

651 Adams Timpani
13814 Lookout Road
San Antonio TX 78233

652 Allied Music Corporation
P.O. Box 288
Elkhorn WI 53121

653 American Way Marketing
P.O. Box 1681
Elkhart IN 46515

654 Ardsley Musical Instrument
Company
165 Broadway
Hastings-on-Hudson NY 10706

655 Armstrong Woodwinds
P.O. Box 787
Elkhart IN 46515

656 Artley Woodwinds
1000 Industrial Parkway
Elkhart IN 46516

657 Avedis Zildjian Co.
22 Longwater Drive
Norwell MA 02061

Bach *see* Selmer Company

658 Bandstand, Inc.
9222 Broadway
Brookfield IL 60513

659 Barclay-Winston Instruments
38-44 W. 21st Street
New York NY 10010

660 Bay Woodwind Products
P.O. Box 3935
Westlake Village CA 91361

661 Benge Professional Brass
c/o United Musical Instruments U.S.A., Inc.
P.O. Box 727
Elkhart IN 46515
Includes trumpets

662 Boosey & Hawkes/Buffet
Crampon, Inc.
1925 Enterprise Court
Libertyville IL 60048

663 Brannen Brothers—Flutemakers, Inc.
58 Dragon Court
Woburn MA 01801

664 Calato/Regal Tip
4501 Hyde Park Blvd.
Niagara Falls NY 14305

665 Calicchio Trumpets
6409 Willoughby Avenue
Hollywood CA 90038

666 Cincinnati Fluteworks
621 Clemmer Ave., #13
Clifton Heights
Cincinnati OH 45219

667 Civil and Military Arts, Ltd.
Amersham, England
Makes gear by hand and paints equipment and instruments (e.g., drums)

668 Conn Band Instruments
P.O. Box 727

Elkhart, IN 46515
Offers tuba conversion tube marching accessory kit

669 DEG Music Products, Inc.
Highway H North
P.O. Box 968
Lake Geneva WI 53147

670 Drelinger Flute Mouthpiece
Company
P.O. Box 146
N. White Plains NY

671 Drum Heaven
P.O. Box 1831
Jamaica Plain MA 02129

672 Drum Workshops
101 Bernoulli Circle
Oxnard CA 93030

673 Drums Ltd. (A. Bill Crowden's)
222 S. Jefferson
Chicago IL 60661

674 Drums Unlimited Inc.
4928 St. Elmo Avenue
Bethesda MD 20814

Dynasty Eagle Marching Percussion *see* DEG Music Products, Inc.

675 Edmund's Double Reeds
12513 Parker Lane
Clinton MO 64735

676 Edward Almeida Flutes
17 Arrowhead Drive
Tiverton RI 02878

E.M. Winston Band Instruments
see Barclay-Winston Instruments

Opposite: *Uptown String Band, Philadelphia PA.*

677 Emerson Musical Instruments,
    Inc.
    611 Eisenhauer Street
    Grand Junction CO 81505

678 F.E. Olds & Son, Inc.
    Distribution and Warranty
    Center
    P.O. Box 1130
    Mountainside NJ 07092

679 Flute World
    29920 Orchard Lake Road
    Farmington Hills MI 48334

Frank's Drum Shop, Inc. *see*
    Drums Ltd.

680 G. Leblanc Corporation
    7001 Leblanc Blvd.
    Kenosha WI 53141-1415

681 G. Pruefer Manufacturing
    Company, Inc.
    1669 Hartford Avenue
    Johnston RI 02919

682 Gemeinhardt Company, Inc.
    P.O. Box 788
    57882 State Road 19 South
    Elkhart IN 46515

683 Geneva International Corpora-
    tion
    29 East Hintz Road
    Wheeling IL 60090

684 Getzen Company
    530 S. Highway H
    Elkhorn WI 53121

685 Giardinelli Band Instruments
    Company
    7845 Maltage Drive
    Liverpool NY 13088

686 Hardy's Musical Instrument
    Company, Inc.
    30462 C.R. 12 West
    Elkhart IN 46514

687 Hayes House of Music
    2011 W. 6th Street
    Topeka KS 66606

688 Interstate Music Supply
    P.O. Box 315
    13819 W. National Avenue
    New Berlin WI 53151

689 Jupiter Band Instruments, Inc.
    P.O. Box 90249
    Austin TX 78709-0249

690 Kaman Music Corporation
    P.O. Box 507
    Bloomfield CT 06002

691 Kanstul Musical Instruments
    1332 S. Claudina
    Anaheim CA 92805

692 King Musical Instruments
    P.O. Box 787
    Elkhart IN 46515

693 Latin Percussion, Inc.
    160 Belmont Avenue
    Garfield NJ 07026

694 Ludwig Industries
    Box 310
    Elkhart IN 46515

695 Malmark, Inc.
    Bell Crest Park
    Plumsteadville PA 18949
        Handbells

696 Miyazawa Flutes USA
    1214 Fifth Street
    Coralville IA 52241

697 Musicrafts International, Inc.
    4111 Todd Lane
    Austin TX 78744
        Sells Jupiter wind instruments
        and percussion

Musser (vibes) *see* Selmer Company

698 National Educational Music
    Company, Ltd.
    1181 Route 22
    Box 1130
    Mountainside NJ 07092

699 National Music, Inc.
    826 Massachusetts Avenue
    Arlington MA 02174

700 National Music Supply of
    Florida
    P.O. Box 1421
    St. Petersburg FL 33733

701 Orpheus Music
    13814 Lookout Road
    San Antonio TX 78233

702 Paiste America, Inc.
    460 Atlas St.
    Brea CA 92621
       Cymbals, gongs, chimes

703 Pearl Corporation
    549 Metroplex Drive
    P.O. Box 111240
    Nashville TN 37211

704 The Percussion Center & Mu-
    sic Spectrum
    1701 North Harrison Street
    Fort Wayne IN 46802

705 Philip Muncy Woodwinds
    RR 4, Box 174B
    Banner Elk NC 28604

706 Premier Percussion USA, Inc.
    1263 Glen Avenue, Suite 250
    Moorestown NJ 08057

PRO-MARK *see* REMO, Inc.

707 Rayburn Musical Instrument
    Company, Inc.
    263 Huntington Avenue
    Boston MA 02115

708 REMO, Inc.
    12804 Raymer Street
    North Hollywood CA 91605
       Drums

709 Ross Mallet Instruments, Inc.
    1304 First Avenue
    Chippewa Falls WI 54729

710 Sabian Ltd.
    Meductic
    New Brunswick E0H 1L0
    Canada
       Cymbals, gongs

711 Saga Musical Instruments
    Box 2841
    South San Francisco CA
       Includes Celtic instruments

712 Sam Ash Music
    2100 Route 38
    Cherry Hill NJ 08002 (Plus
    other locations)

713 Saxophone Shop, Ltd.
    2834 Central St.
    Evanston IL 60201

714 Schilke Music, Inc.
    4520 James Place
    Melrose Park IL 60160

715 Schulmerich Carillons, Inc.
    Carillon Highway
    Sellersville PA 18960

716 Selmer Company
    P.O. Box 310
    Elkhart IN 46515
       Distributes Bach brass instru-
       ments

717 Stingray Percussion
    1228-B 53rd Street
    Mangonia Park FL 33407

718 Tradewinds
    2733 Shelter Island Drive, #303

San Diego CA 92101
Flutes

719 United Musical Instruments
U.S.A., Inc.
1000 Industrial Parkway
P.O. Box 727
Elkhart IN 46515
Distributes Benge trumpets,
King trombones and trum-
pets

720 Verne Q. Powell Flutes, Inc.
257 Crescent Street
Waltham MA 02154

721 Wenger Corporation
555 Park Drive
Owatonna MN 55060

Western Music Specialty Company
see Roper Music

722 Westwind Musical Products
1214 5th Street
Coralville IA 52241

723 Wichita Band Instrument
Company, Inc.
2525 E. Douglas
Wichita KS 67211

724 Wm. S. Haynes Company,
Inc.
12 Piedmond Street
Boston MA 02116

725 Williams Flutes
1165R Massachusetts Avenue
Arlington Ma 02174

726 Woodwind & the Brasswind
19880 State Line Road
South Bend IN 46637

727 Yamaha Corporation of Amer-
ica
Band & Orchestral Division
3445 East Paris Ave. S.E.
P.O. Box 899
Grand Rapids MI 49512

Instrument Accessories

728 Aerospace Lubricants, Inc.
1505 Delashmut Ave.
Columbus OH
Includes Alisyn Valve, Slide
and Key Oil

729 A-K Medical Software
P.O. Box 50329
Columbia SC 29250
Brace Guard orthodontic
embouchure aid

730 Altieri Instrument Bags
5 South Fox Street
Denver CO 80221

731 Archives
210 Route 109
P.O. Box J
E. Farmingdale NY 11735
Music writing paper

732 Arundo Reed & Cane
Rt. 3, Box 298
Hillsboro OR 97124

733 Gripmaster
IMC Prod Corp.
100A Tec Street
Hicksville NY 11801
Finger exercises

Opposite: *Claymont High School Flaming Arrow Alumni Band, Delaware.*

734 Hamilton Stands
Krauth & Benninghofen Company
Hamilton OH 45012

735 J. D'Addario & Company, Inc.
P.O. Box J (210 Rt. 109)
East Farmingdale NY 11735
Vandoren reeds

736 Jet-Tone, Inc.
P.O. Box 1462
Elkhart IN 46515
Mouthpieces

Jo-Ral Mutes *see* Selmer Company

737 JTG of Nashville
1024-C 18th Avenue South
Nashville TN 37212

738 Kombo Cart International
P.O. Box 837
Orem UT 84059

739 L-S Music Innovations
250 H Street, Suite 8110
Department 718
Blaine WA 98230

740 Ludwig
P.O. Box 310
Elkhart IN 46515
Snare & Bell Paks

741 McFarland Double Reed Shop
Dept. I
P.O. Box 13505
Atlanta GA 30324

742 Marlin Lesher Reed, Inc.
P.O. Box 163
Randolph NY 14772

743 Mitchell Lurie
2277 Pelham Avenue
Los Angeles CA 90064
Mouthpiece

744 MMB Music, Inc.
10370 Page Industrial Blvd.
St. Louis MO 63132

745 Neill Sanders Mouthpieces
186 Podunk Lake Road
Hastings MI 49058

746 Olathe Band Instrument
13260 Lakeshore
Olathe KS 66061
Flute bags

747 Peterson Electro-Musical
Products, Inc.
11601 South Mayfield Avenue
Worth IL 60482
Strobe tuners, ear training devices

748 PRO MARK Corporation
10707 Craighead
Houston TX 77025
Drumsticks

749 Rascher Saxophone Mouthpieces
6335 Mayfair Drive
Clarence Center NY 14032

750 RIA
P.O. Box 010359
Staten Island NY 10301
Saxophone & clarinet mouthpieces

751 RICO International
8484 San Fernando Road
Sun Valley CA 91352
Reeds

752 Roland Corporation
7200 Dominion Circle
Los Angeles CA 90040
Tuners

753 S and H Manufacturing Co.
316 W. Summit St.
Normal IL 61761
Instrument racks

754 Seiko
c/o Kaman Music Corporation
P.O. Box 507
Bloomfield CT 06002
Tuners

755 Sounds of Woodwinds
Box 91
Hancock MA 01237

756 Stork Custom Mouthpieces
Rt. 2, Box 1818
Maple Hill Road
Plainfield VT 05667

757 Superslick Products
c/o American Way Marketing

P.O. Box 1681
Elkhart IN 46515
Trombone slide oil

Tru-Vu Transparent Mouthpieces
see L-S Music Innovations

Vandoren of Paris (reeds, mouthpieces) *see* J. D'Addario & Co.,
Inc.

758 Wenger Corporation
P.O. Box 448
Owatonna MN 55060
SousaSaver grandstand bench
mount; Halftime TM compu-
terized charting for marching
bands

Instrument Repair

759 Cincinnati Fluteworks
621 Clemmer Avenue, #13
Clifton Heights
Cincinnati OH 45219

760 Conn Band Instruments
P.O. Box 727
Elkhart IN 46515

761 Flute Specialists, Inc.
120 W. 11 Mile Road, Suite 12
Royal Oak MI 48067

762 Take Care
P.O. Box 73266
Puyallup WA 98373-0266
Video tapes on maintenance

763 Woodwind Repair and Sales
414 Evergreen Avenue
Bradley Beach NJ 07720

Uniform and Footwear
Manufacturers and Distributors

Note: The Instrumentalist *contains a classified section in*
which schools offer old uniforms for sale.

764 Artcraft Blazers
7502 Thomas Street
Pittsburgh PA 15201

765 Ashley Company
10 Harold Street
Sylva NC 28779

Alexis I. DuPont High School Tiger Marching Band, Greenville, Delaware.

Caravel Academy Buccaneer Marching Band, Bear, Delaware.

766 Assured Growth Industries
1702 Fairmont
Mechanicsburg PA 17055

767 Band Mans Company
3328 Towerwood Drive
Dallas TX 75234

768 Bayly, Inc.
4151 N. 29th Ave.
Hollywood FL 33020

769 Colorifics
P.O. Box 26657
Columbus OH 43226
Auxiliary units

770 Cote Inc.
74 W. Bridge Street
Morrisville PA 19067

771 DeMoulin Bros. & Co.
1000 S. 4th Street
Greenville IL 62246

Includes drum major uniform
program

Dinkle Vanguard marching shoe
see Assured Growth Industries

772 Drillmasters
251 West 74th St.
New York NY 10023

Drillstar Company *see* Drillmasters

773 Ebert Sportswear Manufacturing
5000 Fernandina Road
Columbia SC 29212

774 Ed Jameson & Associates
2127 N. Genesee Road
Burton MI 48509
Shoes, flags, gloves, etc.

775 Fechheimer Bros. Company
4545 Malsbary Road
Cincinnati OH 45242

776 Foxx Manufacturing
5199 E. Mahoning Ave.
Warren OH 44483
Has Otterwear Rainwear

777 Fruhauf Uniforms, Inc.
P.O. Box 16159
Wichita KS 67216-6159

778 Gotham Shoe Co. Inc.
P.O. Box 1629
Binghamton NY 13902

779 Hayden School Supply
P.O. Box 27777
Tempe AZ 85285

780 Intermedia, Inc.
85 Carver Avenue
Westwood NJ 07675

781 Jiffy Band Uniforms
Division Richards Jiffy Uni-
forms
One North Alex Road
Dayton OH 45449

782 Merchants Uniform Manufacturing Inc.
7520 E. Colfax Avenue
Denver CO 80203

783 Nicsinger Uniform Company
(purchased by Band Mans
Company)

784 Palombo Uniforms, Inc.
123 Edgewood Avenue
Pittsburgh PA 15218

785 Peacock's Marching World
1200-A N. Jefferson St.
Anaheim CA 92807

786 Raeford Uniform Fabrics
1345 Avenue of the Americas
New York NY 10105

787 SEFCO Plumes
Kerr's Music World
911 Bigley Avenue
Charleston WV 25302

788 Sol Frank Uniforms, Inc.
702 S. Santa Rosa
San Antonio TX 78204

789 Stanbury Uniforms
P.O. Box 100
Brookfield MO 64628

790 Taffy's on Parade
701 Beta Drive
Cleveland OH 44143

791 Wear-A-Knit Corporation
1306 18th Street
Cloquet MN 55720

792 Zoro Corporation
2434 Brockton
San Antonio TX 78217
Sportshirts, jackets

Selected Bibliography

Articles

793 Beckwith, Gene, and Huth, John. "Cleaning Piston Valve Instruments."
Instrumentalist (July 1988): 26–28, 30.

794 Fonder, Mark. "The Instrument Manufacturing Industry and the School
Band Movement: A Look at the 'Holton School Band Plan.'" *Journal
of Band Research* (Fall 1988): 44–51.

795 Harris, Wilbur C. "Ten Repairs Every Band Director Should Know." *School Musician, Director & Teacher* (April 1981): 16.

796 Healy, Guinevere. "Tuba in the Tub: A Guide to Cleaning." *Instrumentalist* (November 1992): 28, 40, 42.

797 McKinney, James. "Percussion Accessories You Can Make." *Instrumentalist* (April 1983): 46–48.

798 Page, Nick. "Guide to Purchasing Band Uniforms." *Instrumentalist* (February 1988): 66, 68, 70–72.

799 Sperl, Gary. "Woodwind Instrument Maintenance." *Music Educators Journal* (March 1980): 46.

800 Von Bergen, Elizabeth F. "Careers in Manufacturing and Merchandising." *Instrumentalist* (August 1977): 44–48.

Books

801 Brand, Erick D. *Selmer Band Instrument Repairing Manual.* 4th ed. Elkhart IN: H. & A. Selmer, 1946.

802 *Care of Band Instruments.* Grand Rapids MI: York Band Instrument Company, 1940.

Henderson High School Warrior Marching Band, West Chester, PA.

803 Meyer, R.F. *The Band Director's Guide to Instrument Repair.* Port Washington NY: Alfred Publishing Company, 1973.

804 Mueller, Kenneth A. *A Complete Guide to the Maintenance and Repair of Band Instruments.* West Nyack NY: Parker Publishing Company, 1982.

805 Springer, George H. *Maintenance and Repair of Wind and Percussion Instruments.* Boston MA: Allyn and Bacon, 1976.

806 Tiede, Clayton H. *The Practical Band Instrument Repair Manual.* Dubuque IA: William C. Brown, 1976.

Indoor Color Guard, West Chester University, West Chester, PA.

Part 8
Music Selection

The following music has been used successfully by indoor color guards, marching bands, and dance-twirl squads.

Color Guard

Entrance/Exit Numbers

807 "America" (Neil Diamond, *The Jazz Singer* soundtrack)

808 "Another Brick in the Wall" (Pink Floyd)

809 "Baker Street" (Gerry Rafferty)

810 "The Break-Up Song" (Greg Kihn Band)

811 "Celebration" (Kool and the Gang)

812 "The Empire Strikes Back" (theme from movie soundtrack)

813 "Games People Play" (Alan Parsons Project)

814 "Kyrie" (Mr. Mister)

815 "Looks Like We Made It" (Barry Manilow)

816 "More Than a Feeling" (Boston)

817 "Nobody Does It Better" (Carly Simon)

818 "Relight My Fire" (Dan Hartman)

819 "Ride Like the Wind" (Christopher Cross)

820 "Rockford Files" (TV theme)

821 "September" (Earth, Wind & Fire)

822 "Sometimes a Fantasy" (Billy Joel)

823 "The Tide Is High" (Blondie)

824 "Turn It On Again" (Genesis)

825 "We Are the Champions" (Queen)

Performance Numbers

826 "All Night Long" (Lionel Ritchie)

827 "American Salute" (Morton Gould)

828 "Another Cha-Cha" (Santa Esmeralda)

829 "Bacchanal from Samson and Delilah" (Saint-Saens)

830 "Birdland" (Manhattan Transfer; arr. Zawinul/Lowden)

831 "Captain from Castile" (theme from movie soundtrack)

832 "Carmen" (Bizet)

833 "Carry On Wayward Son" (Kansas)

834 "Casino Royale" (theme from movie soundtrack)

Thomas McKean High School Highlander Marching Band, Wilmington, Delaware.

835 "Celebration" (Kool and the Gang)

836 "Center Field" (John Fogarty)

837 "Cheeseburger in Paradise" (Jimmy Buffett)

838 "Classical Gas" (Mason Williams)

839 "Come Sail Away" (Styx)

840 "Conga" (Miami Sound Machine)

841 "Copacabana" (Barry Manilow)

842 "Devil Went Down to Georgia" (Charlie Daniels Band)

843 "Don't Cry" (Asia)

844 "Don't Hold Back Your Love" (Daryl Hall)

845 "Don't Let Me Be Misunderstood" (Santa Esmeralda)

846 "Dreamer" (Supertramp)

847 "Funeral for a Friend/Love Lies Bleeding" (Elton John)

848 "Getaway" (Earth, Wind & Fire)

849 "Ghost Riders in the Sky" (Gene Autry)

850 "Hands Down" (Dan Hartman)

851 "Hitman" (AB Logig)

852 "Holding Out for a Hero" (Bonnie Tyler)

853 "Hot, Hot, Hot/Ole, Ole" (Sam Wright)

854 "In the Stone" (arr. Horney, Gilboe)

855 "In Your Eyes" (Peter Gabriel)

856 "It's Raining Men" (Weather Girls)

857 "Joy" (Switched on Bach)

858 "Kokomo" (Beach Boys)

859 "Lady in Red" (Chris De Burgh)

860 "Late in the Evening" (Paul Simon)

861 "Live and Let Die" (theme from movie soundtrack)

862 "Long Time" (Boston)

863 "Lost Boys" (theme from movie soundtrack)

864 "Manhattan Skyline" (*Saturday Night Fever* soundtrack)

865 "Miss Saigon" (Broadway cast album)

866 "More Than a Feeling" (Boston)

867 "Mountain Music" (Alabama)

868 "Music Is My First Love" (Don Miles)

869 "Night on Bald Mountain" (Mussorgsky)

870 "Paradise Theater" (Styx)

871 "Peace of Mind" (Boston)

872 "Piano Man" (Billy Joel)

873 "Pressure" (Billy Joel)

874 "Ride-O-Rocket" (Brothers Johnson)

875 "Rocky" (theme from movie soundtrack)

876 "Shaft" (theme from movie soundtrack)

877 "Ships" (Barry Manilow)

878 "Star Wars" (theme from movie soundtrack)

879 "Starlight Express" (Broadway cast album)

880 "Superman" (theme from movie soundtrack)

881 "Tomorrow" (theme from *Annie* soundtrack/Broadway cast album)

882 "Turn It On Again" (Genesis)

883 "Under Pressure" (Queen/David Bowie)

884 "We're in the Money" (theme from *Gold Diggers of 1993* soundtrack)

Marching Band Field Show/Parade Numbers

885 "Alexander's Ragtime Band" (arr. Bocook; Jenson)

886 "An American in Paris" (arr. Snoeck; McCormick's)

887 "Aztec Fire" (arr. Bocook; Jenson)

888 "Beauty and the Beast" (arr. Lavender; Jenson; arr. Bocook, Jenson)

889 "Bellavia" (arr. Mangione/ Holcombe; Warner Bros.)

890 "Big Noise from Winnetka" (arr. Michael Sweeney and J.J. Jenkins; Warner Bros.)

891 "Birdland" (arr. Snoeck; Barnhouse)

892 "Brian's Song" (arr. Cotter; Columbia/Jenson)

894 "Carmen Overture" (arr. Ahronheim; Presser)

895 "Carmina Burana" (arr. Roberson; Warner Bros.)

896 "Colonel Bogey" (arr. Burns; CPP/Belwin)

897 "Come In from the Rain" (arr. Bocook; Jenson)

898 "Copacabana" (arr. Vinson; Warner Bros.)

899 "Crown Imperial" (arr. Bocook; Jenson)

900 "Don't Cry for Me, Argentina" (arr. Edmondson; Leeds/ MCA)

901 "Ease on Down the Road" (percussion; arr. Rapp; Jenson)

902 "1812 Overture" (arr. Jurrens; Jenson)

903 "Endless Love" (arr. Kerchner; Hal Leonard)

904 "Fantasy" (arr. Jennings; Jenson)

905 "Feels So Good" (arr. Mangione; CPP/Belwin)

906 "La Fiesta" (arr. Corea/ Ahronheim; Warner Bros.)

907 "Firebird" (arr. Bocook; Jenson)

908 "El Gato Triste" (arr. Kerchner/Tuthill; Hal Leonard)

909 "Great Gate of Kiev" (arr. Salzman; Columbia; arr. Dawson; Arrangers' Pub. Co. — corps style)

910 "I Write the Songs" (arr. Higgins; Jenson)

911 "If You Believe" (arr. Smalls/ Bocook; Columbia/Jenson)

912 "In the Midnight Hour" (arr. Waters; Hal Leonard)

913 "James Bond 007 Theme" (arr. Dye; CPP/Belwin)

914 "Lassus Trombone" (arr. Moffit; Hal Leonard)

915 "Layla" (arr. Bocook; Hal Leonard)

916 "Let It Be Me" (arr. Curtis, De Lanoe, Becaud/Ott, Cahill; Hal Leonard)

917 "Long and Winding Road" (arr. Pegram; Hal Leonard)

918 "The Magnificent Seven" (arr. Bullock; Belwin)

919 "Malaguena" (arr. Higgins or Sweeney; Hal Leonard)

920 "Marriage of Figaro" (arr. Balent; Jenson)

921 "The Muppet Show" (percussion; arr. Rapp; Jenson)

922 "New World Symphony" (arr. Bocook; Jenson); (arr. Story; CPP/Belwin)

923 "Night on Bald Mountain" (arr. Wanamaker; Alfred)

924 "Noel" (Cal Danielson/Mid-America Music Publisher)

925 "Ol' Man River" (arr. Moffit; Hal Leonard)

926 "Olympic Fanfare and Theme" (arr. Lavender; Warner Bros.)

927 "On Broadway" (arr. Lavender; Jenson)

928 "Overture from Candide" (arr. Grundmun; Boosey & Hawkes)

929 "Peg" (arr. Higgins; Jenson)

930 "Phantom of the Opera" (arr. Vinson; Hal Leonard)

931 "Pictures at an Exhibition" (arr. Bocook; Jenson)

932 "(I've Been Working on the) Railroad" (William Ballenger/Mid-America Music Publishers)

933 "Ready to Take a Chance Again" (arr. Bocook; Jenson)

934 "Ride Like the Wind" (arr. Tim Waters; Hal Leonard)

935 "Russian Christmas Music" (arr. Hopper; Barnhouse)

936 "Russian Sailor's Dance" (arr. Walters; William Allen)

937 "Saints (Go Marching In)" (arr. Walters; Hal Leonard)

938 "Salute to Sousa!" (Neil Boumpani/Mid-America Music Publishers)

939 "Semper Fi" (arr. Bocook; Jenson)

940 "Send in the Clowns" (arr. Sondheim/Higgins; Jenson)

941 "Shaker Hymn" (arr. Taylor; Columbia)

942 "Shenandoah" (arr. Downey/Rapp; Jenson)

943 "Sing, Sing, Sing" (arr. Moffitt; Hal Leonard)

944 "Slaughter on Tenth Avenue" (arr. Rodgers/Kerchner; Hal Leonard)

945 "Softly As I Leave You" (arr. DeVita/Kerchner, Cahill; Hal Leonard)

946 "Sport" (Cal Danielson/Mid-America Music Publishers)

947 "Star" (arr. Cotter; Jenson)

948 "StarDate" (arr. Brinkman; Mid-America Music Publishers)

949 "The Stars and Stripes Forever" (arr. Smith; Jenson)

950 "Strike Up the Band" (arr. Dye; Warner Bros.)

951 "Superman Theme" (arr. Cotter; Jenson/Warner Bros.)

952 "Swamp Boogie" (David Brinkman/Mid-America Music Publishers)

953 "Swan Lake" (arr. Pegram; Hal Leonard)

954 "Swanee River/Camptown Races" (David Brinkman/Mid-America Music Publishers)

955 "Sweet Georgia Brown" (arr. Will Rapp and Paul Jennings; Jenson)

956 "Take the 'A' Train" (arr. Higgins; Jenson)

957 "Temptation" (arr. Bocook; Jenson)

958 "Terminator 2" (arr. Michael Sweeney; Hal Leonard)

959 "They're Playing Our Song" (arr. Nowak; Hal Leonard)

960 "Through the Eyes of Love" (arr. Hamlisch/Cotter; Jenson/Columbia)

961 "T J" (David Brinkman/Mid-America Music Publishers)

962 "Tomorrow" (arr. Jennings; Jenson)

963 "Twelfth Street Rag" (arr. Higgins; Jenson)

964 "Twilight Zone" (arr. Higgins; Jenson)

965 "Under the Sea" (arr. Will Rapp; Jenson)

966 "Veracruz" (arr. Bocook; Jenson)

967 "Victors" (Jeff James/Mid-America Music Publishers)

968 "The Way We Were" (arr. McCullough; Columbia)

969 "Weekend in New England" (arr. Edelman/Scott; Warner Bros.)

970 "What I Did for Love" (arr. Edmonson; Hal Leonard)

971 "A Whole New World" (arr. Bocook; Jenson)

972 "Yankee Doodle Dandy" (Cal Danielson/Mid-America Music Publishers)

973 "You'll Never Walk Alone" (arr. Kerchner; Hal Leonard)

974 "You're a Grand Old Flag" (arr. Moffitt; Hal Leonard)

975 "You've Lost That Lovin' Feelin'" (arr. Cotter; Jenson)

Twirling Selections (Group Dance-Twirl)

Entrance/Exit Numbers

976 "Alive Again" (Chicago)

977 "Girls Just Want to Have Fun" (Cyndi Lauper)

978 "Had Enough" (The Who)

979 "I Love Rock and Roll" (Joan Jett & the Blackhearts)

980 "Jet Airliner" (Steve Miller)

981 "Music Box Dancer" (Frank Mills)

982 "On Broadway" (George Benson)

983 "Rise" (Herb Alpert)

984 "Stony End" (Barbra Streisand)

985 "What I Did for Love" (*A Chorus Line* cast album)

Performance Numbers

986 "All That Jazz" (Chicago)

987 "Beat It" (Michael Jackson)

988 "Best of My Love" (Emotions)

989 "Brand New Day" (The Wiz)

990 "Breaking Away" (Balance)

991 "Bye Bye Birdie" (theme from movie soundtrack)

992 "Can-Can" (arr. Wanamaker; Alfred)

993 "Celebration" (Kool and the Gang)

994 "City Lights" (Liza Minnelli)

995 "Danger Zone" (Kenny Loggins)

996 "Desdemona" (from *Fame* soundtrack)

997 "Don't Stop Till You Got Enough" (Michael Jackson)

998 "Ease on Down the Road" (from *The Wiz* soundtrack/ Broadway cast album)

999 "Fame" (theme from movie soundtrack; Irene Cara)

1000 "Hands Down" (Dan Hartman)

1001 "Hawaii 5-0" (TV theme; Ventures)

1002 "Hip to Be Square" (Huey Lewis and the News)

1003 "Hit Me with Your Best Shot" (Pat Benatar)

1004 "House of the Rising Sun" (Eric Burdon and the Animals)

1005 "I'm Coming Out" (Diana Ross)

1006 "Jailhouse Rock" (Elvis Presley)

Opposite: *Chesapeake Indoor Color Guard, Maryland.*

1007 "Jump" (Van Halen)

1008 "Jump" (Pointer Sisters)

1009 "Jump Shout Boogie" (Barry Manilow)

1010 "Knock on Wood" (Aretha Franklin)

1011 "Theme from *Ladyhawke*" (soundtrack)

1012 "Let's Hear It for Me" (Barbra Streisand)

1013 "Love Is a Battlefield" (Pat Benatar)

1014 "MacArthur Park" (Donna Summer)

1015 "The Main Event" (theme from movie soundtrack; Barbra Streisand)

1016 "Makin' It" (from *Meatballs* soundtrack; David Naughton)

1017 "Manhattan Skyline" (from *Saturday Night Fever* soundtrack)

1018 "The Music and the Mirror" (from *A Chorus Line* cast album)

1019 "New York City Rhythm" (Barry Manilow)

1020 "Once Upon a Time" (Donna Summer)

1021 "Ring My Bell" (Anita Ward)

1022 "Rio" (Peter Allen)

1023 "Rootbeer Rag" (Billy Joel)

1024 "Scotch Machine" (Marlin, "Voyage" album; T.K. Productions, Hialeah FL)

1025 "Spies in the Night" (Manhattan Transfer)

1026 "They're Playing Our Song" (from Broadway cast album)

1027 "A View to a Kill/Dance into the Fire" (theme from movie soundtrack; Duran Duran)

1028 "Viva Las Vegas" (Elvis Presley)

1029 "Walk Him Up the Stairs" (*Purlie* cast album)

1030 "Working for the Weekend" (Loverboy)

1031 "Yankee Doodle Boy" (DCA Experience, Bicentennial Gold Album; Private Stock Records)

1032 "You Should Be Dancing" (from *Saturday Night Fever* soundtrack)

1033 "You're the One That I Want" (from *Grease* soundtrack)

Music Libraries and Research Centers

1034 American Bandmasters Association Research Center
Fine Arts Department
McKeldin Library
University of Maryland
College Park MD 20742

1035 American Music Center
30 W. 26th Street, Suite 1001
New York NY 10010-2011

1036 Chatfield Brass Band Music
Lending Library
81 Library Lane
P.O. Box 578
Chatfield MN 55923

Music Publishers and Distributors

1037 Alfred Publishing Company, Inc.
16380 Roscoe Blvd.
P.O. Box 10003
Van Nuys CA 91410-0003 and
487 Westney Rd. South,
Unit #1
Ajax, Ontario L1S 6W7
Canada
or P.O. Box 2355
Taren Point, NSW 2229
Australia

1038 All Star Records
c/o Star Line Baton Company
P.O. Box 5490
Pompano Beach FL 33074-5490

Belwin Mills Publishing Corporation *see* CPP/Belwin, Inc.

1039 Boosey and Hawkes, Inc.
52 Cooper Square
New York NY 10003

1040 Brodt Music Company, Inc.
P.O. Box 9345
Charlotte NC 28299

1041 Broude Brothers, Ltd.
170 Varick Street
New York NY 10013

1042 Carl Fischer, Inc.
62 Cooper Square
New York NY 10003
Carl Fischer Music Distributors
52 Cooper Square
New York NY 10003
or Carl Fischer Music Distributors
312 South Wabash Avenue
Chicago IL 60604
or Carl Fischer of Boston
156 Boylston Street
Boston MA 02116

1043 C.F. Peters Corporation
373 Park Avenue South
New York NY 10016

Chappell & Company *see* Hal Leonard Publishing Corporation

1044 C.L. Barnhouse Company
Music Publishers
Box 680
Oskaloosa IA 52577

Colfranc Music Publishing Corporation *see* CPP/Belwin, Inc.

1046 CPP/Belwin, Inc.
15800 Northwest 48th Avenue
P.O. Box 4340
Miami FL 33014

1047 Drum and Bugle Corps Recordings
P.O. Box 548
Lombard IL 60148-0548

1048 Drummit Publications
33408 Bassett Road
Burlington WI

Edward B. Marks Music Corporation *see* Hal Leonard Publishing Corporation

1049 Edwin F. Kalmus & Company, Inc.
P.O. Box 5011
Boca Raton FL 33431

1050 Elkan-Vogel, Inc.
Presser Place & Lancaster Avenue
Bryn Mawr PA 19010

G. Schirmer, Inc. *see* Hal Leonard Publishing Corporation

Gamble Music Company *see* Carl Fischer of Chicago

1051 Hal Leonard Publishing Corporation
7777 W. Bluemound Road
P.O. Box 13819
Milwaukee WI 53213
Distributes catalogs of Chappell & Co., G. Shirmer, Jenson Publications, Edward B. Marks

1052 Hamar Percussion Publications, Inc.
333 Spring Road
Huntington NY

1053 Highland/Etling Publishing Company
1344 Newport
Long Beach CA

1054 The Hindsley Transcriptions
1 Montclair Road
Urbana IL 61801

1055 International Music Company
5 West 37th Street
New York NY

1056 James F. Chapin
RR 2
Box 1017
Elizabeth Street
Sag Harbor NY

Jenson Publications *see* Hal Leonard Publishing Corporation

1057 J.W. Pepper and Son, Inc.
P.O. Box 850
Valley Forge Pa 19482
Also located in Atlanta, Dallas, Detroit, Los Angeles, Paiges IN, Winston-Salem NC

1058 Kendor Music, Inc.
P.O. Box 278
Delevan NY 14042

1059 Ludwig Music Publishing Company
557 East 140th Street
Cleveland OH 44110-1999

M. Witmark and Sons *see* Warner Brothers Publications, Inc.

1060 Magnamusic-Baton
10370 Page Industrial Blvd.
St. Louis MO 63132

1061 Manhattan Beach Music
1595 East 46th Street
Brooklyn NY 11234

1062 Manhattan Music Publica-
tions, Inc.
Acquired by CPP/Belwin,
Inc.

1063 Marching Percussion Northwest
2510 Debra Drive
Springfield OR 97477

Mercury Music Corporation *see*
Theodore Presser Company

1064 Meredith Music Publications
170 N.E. 33rd Street
Ft. Lauderdale FL 33307

1065 Mid-America Music Publish-
ers
Box 234
Malcolm NE 68402

1066 M.M. Cole Publishing Company
251 East Grand Avenue
Chicago IL 60611

1067 Neil A. Kjos Music Company
4380 Jutland Drive
San Diego CA 92117

1068 Norman Lee Publishing, Inc.
Box 528
Oskaloosa IA 52577

1069 Oxford University Press, Inc.
Music Department
200 Madison Avenue
New York NY 10016

Peer International Corporation *see*
Southern Music Company

1070 Pete Guest Music Company
26705 Lorenz
Madison Heights MI 48071

1071 Publishers Outlet
P.O. Box 40772
Nashville TN 37204

1072 RBC Music Company, Inc.
P.O. Box 29128
San Antonio TX 78229

1073 Songo Music
7188 Cradlerock Way, Suite
138
Columbia MD 21045

1074 Southern Music Company
P.O. Box 329
San Antonio TX 78292

1075 Studio P/R
15800 Northwest 48th Avenue
P.O. Box 4340
Miami FL 33126

1076 Theodore Presser Company
Presser Place
Bryn Mawr PA 19010

1077 TRN Music Publisher
P.O. Box 1076
Ruidoso NM 88345

1078 Twirl House (defunct)
Tulsa OK

1079 Warner Brothers Publications
265 Secaucus Road
Secaucus NJ 07094

1080 Warner/Chappel Music, Inc.
10585 Santa Monica Blvd.
Los Angeles CA 90025

1081 William Allen Music, Inc.
P.O. Box 790
Newington VA 22122

1082 Wingert-Jones Music, Inc.
2026 Broadway
Box 419878
Kansas City MO 64141-6878

Associations

1083 American Music Conference
5140 Avenida Encinas
Carlsbad CA 92008

1084 American Musicians Union
8 Tobin Court
Dumont NJ 07628

1085 American Society of Music
Arrangers & Composers
P.O. Box 11
Hollywood CA 90078

1086 Creative Music Foundation
P.O. Box 671
Woodstock NY 12498

1087 International Horn Society
2220 N. 1400 E.
Provo UT 84604

1088 Music Distributors Association
38 West 21st Street
New York NY 10010-6906

1089 Music Library Association
P.O. Box 487
Canton MA 02021

1090 Music Publishers' Association
of the United States
205 East 42nd Street
New York NY 10017

1091 National Association of
School Music Dealers
4020 McEwen, Ste. 105
Dallas TX 75244-5019

1092 National Music Council
P.O. Box 5551
Englewood NJ 07631

1093 National Music Publishers
Association
205 East 42nd Street
New York NY 10017

Selected Bibliography

Articles

1094 Baker, Richard. "Finding That Old Familiar Tune." *Instrumentalist* (September 1987): 84.

1095 Higgins, John. "How to Buy (and Repair) Marching Band Arrangements." *Instrumentalist* (September 1977): 39–44.

1096 Jenson, Art. "Careers in Educational Music Publishing." *Instrumentalist* (August 1977): 48–50.

1097 "Marching Band Music: Comments from Our New Music Reviewers." *Instrumentalist* (June 1980): 8–10.

1098 Mendyk, Lee A. "The Chatfield Brass Band Free Music Lending Library." *Library Journal* (October 1982): 21.

United States Navy Ceremonial Color Guard and Drill Team, Washington DC.

Books

1099 Benton, Rita, comp. *Directory of Music Libraries. Part 1: Canada and the United States.* Iowa City IA: University of Iowa, 1967.

1100 Instrumentalist Company. *Band Music Guide: Alphabetical Listing of Titles and Composers of All Band Music.* Northfield IL, 1989.

1101 *Music Article Guide.* Philadelphia PA: Information Services. Quarterly.

1102 *Music Index. A Subject-Author Guide to Over 300 Current Periodicals from the U.S., England, Canada & Australia and 19 Non-English Language Countries.* Warren MI: Harmonie Park Press (Information Coordinators, Inc.). Monthly.

1103 Rehrig, William H. *The Heritage Encyclopedia of Band Music: Composers and Their Music.* Edited by Paul E. Bierley. Westerville OH: Integrity Press, 1991.

1104 Smith, Norman, and Stoutamire, Albert. *Band Music Notes.* San Diego CA: Neil A. Kjos Music Company, 1979.

Part 9
Parades

General

Some high school marching bands eschew competitions in favor of halftime show and parades and may gear up for trips to the Rose Bowl Parade or Miss America Parade.

Directory

Parades listed here are the biggest of the big, nationally known, or street competitions exclusive of a field show.

1105 All-American College Marching Band
Entertainment Division
Walt Disney World
Orlando FL 32802

1106 Azalea Festival Parade
The North Carolina Azalea Festival
P.O. Box 51
Wilmington NC 28402

1107 Bowl Games of America
302 West 5400 South, Suite 108
P.O. Box 571187
Salt Lake City UT 84157-1187

Brach's Christmas Parade (Chicago, IL) *see* Bowl Games of America

1108 Bristol 4th of July Parade
Bristol 4th of July Committee
Bristol RI 02809

1109 Cherry Royale Parade
108 W. Grandview Parkway
P.O. Box 141
Traverse City MI 49685
See also: National Cherry Festival Parades

Clearwater Fun 'N Sun (Clearwater FL) *see* Bowl Games of America

Conquistador Festival (Albuquerque Founders' Day Parade, April) *see* Performance Connection

1110 Dairy Days/Rodeo Parade
Richland Area Chamber of Commerce
Box 128
Richland Center WI 53581

Edison Light Parade (Ft. Myers FL) *see* Bowl Games of America

1111 Egleston Children's Christmas Parade
3312 Piedmont Road, Suite 506
Atlanta GA 30305

1112 Englewood Holiday Parade
Englewood City and Chamber of Commerce and Merchants Association
Englewood CO 80110

Everglades Festival (Ft. Lauderdale–Broward County St. Patrick's Day Parade, March) *see* Performance Connection

Penncrest Roaring Lions Marching Band, Media, Pennsylvania.

1113 Festival of Champions
8317 Front Beach Road, Suite 27
Panama City Beach FL 32407

1114 Festival of Music
c/o Fire Department
Cedarburg WI 53012

1115 Festival of the States
c/o Suncoasters
1 Beach Drive S.E.
St. Petersburg FL 33731

1116 Florida Citrus Sports Holiday Music Festival
c/o Citrus Sports Travel
1 Citrus Bowl Place
Orlando FL 32805
(800) 932-6440

Foley's Thanksgiving Day Parade (Houston TX) *see* Bowl Games of America

1117 Freedom Festival Marching Parade Contest
c/o C. Herberft Duncan
702 Chatlet Woods
Ferguson MO 63135

1118 Grand Jubilee Carnival Krewes Parade
Memphis Area Chamber of Commerce
P.O. Box 224
Memphis TN 38101

1119 Great Citrus Parade
c/o Circus World Museum
426 Water Street
Baraboo WI 53913

1120 Harvest Festival Grand Feature Parade
Richmond VA 23232

Hollywood Christmas Parade (Hollywood CA) *see* Bowl Games of America

Hyack Festival and Parade (Vancouver, British Columbia) *see* Bowl Games of America

1121 Jack Frost Parade
c/o Lancaster Jaycees
P.O. Box 1118
Lancaster PA 17608

Jr. Orange Bowl Parade (Coral Gables FL) *see* Bowl Games of America

Kentucky Derby Festival Parade *see* Pegasus Parade

1122 King Frost Parade
c/o Hamburg Jaycees
P.O. Box 171
Hamburg PA 19526

Klondike Days (Edmonton, Alberta, Canada) *see* Bowl Games of America

1123 McDonald's All-American High School Band
P.O. Box 11189
Chicago IL 60611

1124 McDonald's Charity Christmas Parade (Chicago IL)
c/o Bands of America
P.O. Box 665
Arlington Heights IL 60006
(312) 398-7270

1125 (Macy's) Thanksgiving Day Parade
151 West 34th Street, 19th Floor
New York NY 10001

1126 Mastercard/WPVI-TV 6 Thanksgiving Parade
Parade Office
4100 City Line Avenue
Philadelphia PA 19131

Michigan Thanksgiving Parade (Detroit) *see* Bowl Games of America

1127 Miss America Pageant Parade
1325 on the Boardwalk
Atlantic City NJ 08401
or P.O. Box 119
Atlantic City NJ 08404

1128 Music in the Parks
1784 West Schuylkill Road
Douglassville PA 19518
Locations: Kings Dominion, Doswell WV; Valleyfair, Shakopee MN; Astroworld, Houston TX; Old Country Busch Gardens, Williamsburg VA; Canada's Wonderland, Toronto, Canada; Cedar Point, Sandusky OH; Dorney Park, Allentown PA; Six Flags Great Adventure, Jackson NJ: Six Flags Great America, Gurnee IL; Great America, Santa Clara CA; Hershey Park, Hershey PA; Opryland, Nashville TN; Six Flags Over Georgia, Atlanta GA; Six Flags Magic Mountain, Los Angeles CA; Six Flags Over Mid-America, St. Louis MO; Six Flags Over Texas, Arlington TX.

1129 National Cherry Blossom Festival Parade
Convention and Visitors Bureau
1575 I Street, N.W., Suite 250
Washington DC 20005
or Heritage Festivals
302 West 5400 South, Suite 108
P.O. Box 571187
Salt Lake City UT 84157-1187

1130 National Cherry Festival Parades
P.O. Box 141
108 W. Grandview Parkway
Traverse City MI 49685

1131 Oktober Color Festival
Delavan/Delavan Lake Area Chamber of Commerce
52 E. Walworth Avenue
Delavan WI 53115

1132 Oz Festival Parade
c/o Chesteron High School
651 W. Morgan Avenue
Chesterton IN 46304

1133 Pageant Parade of the Rockies
Pikes Peak or Bust Rodeo Association
c/o Michael Welch
A.G. Edwards Company
19 North Tejon
Colorado Springs CO 80903

1134 Pegasus Parade
Kentucky Derby Festival Committee
137 W. Muhammed Ali Blvd.
Louisville KY 40202

1135 Performance Connection
1289 Dennis Road
Southampton PA 18996

Philadelphia Thanksgiving Parade *see* Mastercard/WPVI-TV 6 Thanksgiving Parade

Pittsfield 4th of July Parade *see* Bowl Games of America

1136 Preble County Pork Festival
c/o Tim H. Miller
P.O. Box 208
Eaton OH 45320

Queen City Festival Findlay Market Opening Day Parade (Cincinnati, April) *see* Performance Connection

1137 St. Patrick's Day Parade
New York Convention and Visitors Bureau

Methacton High School Marching Band, Fairview Village, Pennsylvania.

2 Columbus Circle
New York NY 10019

1138 St. Patrick's Day Parade
Sydney, N.S.W. 2219
Australia

1139 St. Patrick's Week
Irish Tourist Board
757 Third Avenue
New York NY 10017
Parades and competitions in
Galway, Limerick and Dublin, Ireland

Shamrock Festival (San Diego St.
Patrick's Day Parade, March) *see*
Performance Connection

Shannon Development Company,
Ltd. *see* St. Patrick's Week

1140 Shenandoah Apple Blossom
Festival
5 N. Cameron Street
Winchester VA 22601

1141 Spectacle of Bands Parade
c/o David Kohuth
Zo Ashlea Gardens
New Holland PA

1142 Sun Fun Festival Band Competition
Myrtle Beach Area Chamber
of Commerce
P.O. Box 2115
Myrtle Beach SC 29578

1143 Tournament of Roses Parade
Pasadena Tournament of
Roses Association
391 S. Orange Grove Blvd.
Pasadena CA 91184

1144 Tulip Festival
Chamber of Commerce
P.O. Box 36
Orange City IA 51041
Includes street competitions

1145 Tulip Time Parade of Bands
Tulip Time Festival, Inc.
Holland Convention & Visitors Bureau
171 Lincoln Avenue
Holland MI 49423

1146 University of Wisconsin-
Platteville Homecoming
Parade
SAB Homecoming Committee
Student Center
University of Wisconsin-
Platteville
1 University Plaza
Platteville WI 53818-3099
or University of Wisconsin-
Platteville
Alumni Director
417 Karrmann Library
1 University Plaza
Platteville WI 53818-3099

1147 VFW
c/o Bob Brady, Chairman
National Marching Units and
Parade Committee
319 Tadmar Road
Ross Township
Perryville PA 15237

1148 Virginia Poultry Federation
Grand Feature Parade
Virginia Poultry Federation
P.O. Box 552
Harrisonburg VA 22801

1149 V.P. Parade
P.O. Box 1903
St. Louis MO 63118

1150 Westminster Lord Mayor's
Parade and Albert Hall
Performance
c/o Super Holiday Companies, Inc.
DBA Citrus Sports Travel
1 Citrus Bowl Place

Orlando FL 32805
(800) 932-6440

Your Hometown 4th of July Parade (Pittsfield MA) *see* Bowl Games of America

Selected Bibliography

Articles

1151 "Community Action: They Parade and Perform Just for Fun . . . Theirs Every Bit as Much as Yours." *Sunset* (January 1978): 60–61.

1152 Darnall, Josiah. "Rosy Success Stories." *Instrumentalist* (March 1988): 45–46, 48.

1153 Dart, Leslie. "Music of America in Rose Bowl Parade." *School Musician, Director & Teacher* (December 1979): 6–7, 15.

1154 Haney, Ray B. "McDonald's All-American High School Band: They Do It All for Us!" *School Musician, Director & Teacher* (March 1979): 54–55.

1155 Howard, Karol. "Exercises for the Parade Band." *Instrumentalist* (August 1984): 23–25.

1156 Kenney, Edward L. "A.I. [du Pont] Band Steps Off to Another 1st." *News Journal* [Wilmington DE] (December 31, 1991): D1, last page.

1157 _____. "Rose Parade: Walk on the Weary Side." *News Journal* [Wilmington DE] (January 2, 1990): D1, D2.

1158 Lavelle, Mariane P. "One Band's Run for the Roses." *Philadelphia Inquirer Today Magazine* (December 30, 1979): 1, 8–12.

1159 Mundi, Joseph T., and Bradshaw, R. Bruce. "St. Patrick's Week in Ireland: A Band Goes There and Back Again." *Instrumentalist* (December 1981): 14–16.

1160 Pappas, Peter M. "Bowl Parades Again, Again, and Again." *School Musician, Director & Teacher* (August/September 1979): 12–13.

1161 Riordan, Kevin. "CR [Caesar Rodney] Band Struts Stuff in London." *News Journal* [Wilmington DE] (January 2, 1990): D1.

1162 Roth, Edith B. "A Band, a Community, an Event." *American Education* (October 1981): 23–26.

1163 Wright, Al G. "Band Parade Procedures." *Instrumentalist* (March 1965): 82–85.

Books

1164 Bennett, George T. *Street Routines for Marching Band Contests and Public Exhibitions.* Marching Maneuver Series, Vol. V. Chicago IL: Gamble Hinged Music Company, 1938.

1165 Casavant, Albert R. *Street Parade Drills.* San Antonio TX: Southern Music Company, no date.

1166 Dvorak, Raymond F. *The Band on Parade.* New York NY: Carl Fischer, 1937.

1167 Hackney, C.R., and Emerson, Hugh P. *Parade Stunts.* Marching Maneuver Series, Vol. X. Chicago IL: Gamble Hinged Music Company, 1941.

1168 Johnston, Laurence. *Parade Techniques.* Rockville Centre NY: Belwin, 1944.

1169 Lagauskas, Valerie. *Parades: How to Plan, Promote & Stage Them.* New York: Sterling Publishing, 1982. Includes chapter on marching bands.

Part 10
Publicity and Public Relations

The marching activity frequently receives little publicity. Newspapers may not consider music news. Funds for promotion are scarce. Add to this what seems to be either an insularity or lack of concern for the captive audience of parents and friends. Announcers frequently fail to tell spectators a competing unit's hometown and often do not list upcoming contests. Sometimes organizations forbid the use of camcorders and even still cameras. Is this any way to promote the activity?

A publicity chairperson for a high school band boosters' organization will learn through trial and error what will and what will not work to get one's band noticed in the community. The budget may be only $25, which is too little even to cover stamps, envelopes, and other mundane but necessary items.

In theory, a monthly general booster meeting will be covered in the local newspapers. "County Events" sections usually will list such activities. Letters to the editor regarding a particular musical event or letters from boosters praising the school and students might be printed.

Weekly newspapers are likely to print notices and usually a 5" × 7" black and white photograph if submitted. Photos should be submitted for significant events, such as band parents repainting a refreshment stand at the stadium, a trip, area marching band championships, last practice before a halftime show, or benefit performances for injured class members.

It is difficult to tell whether newspaper notices attract people to booster meetings because phone chains and mailing are also used. Labor under the theory that every little bit counts.

Television stations occasionally cover marching activities and it certainly does no harm to contact them. Marching competitions are something of a well-kept secret in most communities, and a television reporter may find them novel and newsworthy.

The band director can obtain publicity by forming brass choirs for Christmas "caroling" around town and by taking senior high band members to the middle schools for recruiting purposes. Slide presentations and videotapes of a band's field show will also generate enthusiasm. Even a mediocre band will look good from the grandstand on a television monitor.

In-house publicity can be achieved by means of a band scrapbook and photo album. Displayed at all booster meetings, it can be held by the publicity chairperson or located in the school library or band director's office. The scrapbook should include photos, newspaper clippings, programs, and any other items relating to the band or its members.

Souderton High School Indoor Color Guard, Souderton, Pennsylvania.

Selected Bibliography

Articles

1170 Abdoo, Frank B. "A Portable Video Tape Recording System for Your Program." *Instrumentalist* (September 1982): 22–25.

1171 Clayton, Nancy. "Television Coverage for High School Bands?" *School Musician, Director & Teacher* (August/September 1979): 16–18.

1172 Ellis, Roger C. "Views from the Sidelines Through the Eye of a Camera." *Drum Corps News.* 7 parts. Oct. 21–Nov. 4, 1981, p. 19; Nov. 25, 1981, p. 4; Dec. 16, 1981, p. 9; Jan. 13, 1982, p. 11; Mar. 17, 1982, p. 10; Mar. 31, 1982, p. 5; Apr. 21, 1982, p. 11.

1173 Gretick, Tony. "Bryan Music Boosters — An Organization That Works." *Instrumentalist* (May 1983): 21–23.

1174 Lautzenheiser, Tim. "Family Affair." *Booster* (November 1982): 5.

1175 Michaels, Arthur J. "Hop Aboard the Music Education Magazine Bandwagon." *Writer's Digest* (April 1981): 39–43.

1176 _____. "Yes, You Too Can Be a Music Director-Photographer." *School Musician, Director & Teacher* (March 1981): 18–19.

1177 Perkins, Charlene A. "Drum Corps Is Worth the Parental Effort." *Drum Corps News,* June 16, 1982, p. 9.

1178 _____. "Now Is a Good Time to Contact the Pillars of the Community." *Drum Corps News,* June 16, 1982, p. 8.

1179 Wenner, Gene C. "Promoting Our School Music Program." *School Musician, Director & Teacher* (October 1980): 12–14.

Books

1180 Ask, Carolyn, comp. *How to Tell Your Story: A Guide to Public Relations.* Columbus OH: Ohio Arts Council (727 E. Main St., 43205), no date.

1181 Gillespie, Lester. *The Use of Publicity in the Public Relations Program of the High-School Instrumental Music Department.* Fullerton CA: F.E. Olds & Son, 1960.

1182 Leibert, Edwin R., and Sheldon, Bernice E. *Handbook of Special Events for Non-Profit Organizations: Tested Ideas for Fund Raising and Public Relations.* New York NY: Association Press, 1976.

1183 Lewis, H.G. *How to Handle Your Own Public Relations.* Chicago IL: Nelson-Hall, 1976.

1184 O'Brien, Richard. *Publicity: How to Get It.* New York NY: Barnes & Noble, 1977.

1185 Selmer, H. & A., Inc. *How to Promote Your Band — A Manual of Public Relations for the Band Director.* Elkhart, IN, 1957.

Part 11

Travel Arrangements

Directory

1186 American Tours & Travel,
Inc.
5401 Kirkman Road, Suite
475
Orlando FL 32819

1187 America's Travel Centre
302 W. 5400 S., Suite 108
Salt Lake City UT 84107

1188 Anne Cottrell Travel Enterprises
40 Wellington Street East,
3rd Floor
Toronto, Ontario
Canada

1189 Associate Consultants for
Education Abroad
12 East 86th Street, Suite 200
New York NY 10028

1190 A.W.O.L. Travel, Inc.
1757 West Broadway St.,
Suite 3
Oviedo FL 32765

1191 Bob Rogers Travel, Inc.
P.O. Box 673
Warrenville IL 60555

1192 Britt Festivals
P.O. Box 1124
Medford OR 97501

1193 Busch Gardens Special Events
Department
P.O. Box 290377
Tampa FL 33687

1194 Classic Tours of New Jersey
560 Stokes Road, Bldg. 13A
Ironstone Village
Medford NJ 08055

1195 C-S Travel Service, Inc./In-
ternational Youth & Music
Festivals

8222 West 95th Street
Hickory Hills IL 60457

1196 Disney Magic Music Days
P.O. Box 3232
Anaheim CA 92803
or P.O. Box 10,020
Lake Buena Vista FL 32830-
0020

1197 Educational Programs
1784 W. Schuylkill Road
Douglassville PA 19518
Sponsors Festivals of Music,
Music in the Parks

1198 Educational Tour Consultants
934 Baker Lane, Suite A
Winchester VA 22603

1199 Encore International
1486 South 1100 East
Salt Lake City UT 84105

1200 Festivals with Creative Arts
Workshop Showcase
107 Boonton Avenue
Kinnelon NJ 07405

1201 Friendship Ambassadors
Foundation
273 Upper Mountain Avenue
Upper Montclair NJ 07043

1202 Homestead Travel
7 West Main Street
P.O. Box 304
Hummelstown PA 17036-0304
Includes bowl game parades
(Cotton Bowl, Fiesta Bowl,
King Orange Bowl, Tourna-
ment of Roses) and interna-
tional competitions

1203 Intropa
1066 Saratoga Avenue, Suite
100

Horizon Indoor Color Guard, Princeton, New Jersey.

San Jose CA 95129
or 4950 Bissonnet Road
Suite 201
Bellaire TX 77401

1204 Irish Travel Board
757 Third Avenue
New York NY 10017

1205 Music Festivals
P.O. Box 142
Boyertown PA 19512
Sites include: Bahamas
(cruise), Mexico (cruise),
Anaheim CA (Freedom
Bowl Festival, December),
San Diego CA, Montreal,
Canada; Washington DC,
Orlando FL, New Orleans
LA, Philadelphia PA

1206 Music Festivals International
P.O. Box 14
Marcellus NY 13108

1207 National Events
(800) 333-4700
Includes continental U.S. locations, Hawaii, Mexico
City, and Bahamas cruise

1208 Norman Travel
1146 E. Alosta Avenue
Glendora CA 91740

1209 North American Music Festivals
P.O. Box 36
50 Brookwood Drive, Suite 1
Carlisle PA 17013
Sites include: Toronto, Canada; Orlando FL, Boston
MA, Hersheypark PA, Vir-
ginia Beach VA

1210 Opryland USA
2802 Opryland Drive, Room
9426
Nashville TN 37214

1211 Pacific Basin Music Festivals
World Projects
P.O. Box 7365
Berkeley CA 94707

1212 Performing Arts Abroad,
Inc.
P.O. Box 844
Kalamazoo MI 49005
Has Director's Travel Plan-
ner

1213 Performing Arts Consultants
P.O. Box 310
46 Chatham Road
Short Hills NJ 07078
Includes Hawaii, Bahamas
cruise, and bowl games (Na-
tional Freedom Bowl Festi-
val, Los Angeles; National
Hall of Fame Bowl Festival,
Tampa; National Peach
Bowl Festival, Atlanta; Sea
World Holiday Bowl, San
Diego)

1214 Sea World Marketing
7007 Seaworld Drive
Orlando FL 32821

1215 Star Travel Services, Inc.
P.O. Box 1270
Bloomington IN 47402

1216 Super Holiday Tours, Inc.
5960 Lakehurst Drive
Orlando FL 32819

1217 Wells Cargo
P.O. Box 728-1011
Elkhart IN 46515
Trailers

Opposite: *Jersey Surf Drum & Bugle Corps, Camden County, New Jersey.*

Selected Bibliography

Articles

1218 Blahnik, Joel. "The Case Against Travel." *Music Educators Journal* (January 1982): 43–45.

1219 Gerardi, J.L. "The Legal Aspects of an Out-of-State Trip." *Instrumentalist* (May 1983): 12–14.

1220 Haas, Lance. "Take Your Band Camping." *School Musician, Director & Teacher* (November 1977): 70.

1221 Neidig, Kenneth L. "Travel Tips from the Professionals." *Instrumentalist* (May 1983): 8–12.

1222 Prentice, Barbara. "On the Road Again." *Instrumentalist* (January 1990): 27–30, 88–90.

1223 Ritter, Sara. "T[win] V[alley] Band Struts Down Main St., Disney World." *Tri County Record* [Berks, Chester, Lancaster PA], April 20, 1993, pp. 1, 23.

1224 Thoms, Paul E. "Is This Trip Really Necessary?" *School Musician, Director & Teacher* (October 1982): 6–7.

1225 Wood, Roy. "Big Tour ... on a Small Budget." *School Musician, Director & Teacher* (October 1982): 8–10.

Part 12

Trophies, Awards, Gifts, Medals and Plaques

Directory

1226 Ampros Trophies
      4270 U.S. Route 1 North
      Monmouth Junction NJ
      08852-1905

1227 Anyone Can Whistle
      P.O. Box 4407
      Kingston NY 12401

1228 Bandribbons, Inc.
      P.O. Box 145
      Monmouth OR 97361

1229 Best Impressions
      348 North 30th Road
      P.O. Box 800
      La Salle IL 61301
          Buttons, pom-pons, mugs,
          cushions

1230 Friendship House
      29313 Clemens Road #2-G
      P.O. Box 450978
      Cleveland OH 44145-0623

1231 Galaxy Enterprises, Inc.
      6808 Laurel Bowie Road
      Bowie MD 20715

1232 Medals & Awards Interna-
      tional
      P.O. Box 14426
      San Antonio TX 78214

1233 The Music Stand
      1 Rockdale Plaza
      Lebanon NH 03102

1234 John Philip Sousa Band
      Award
      c/o Instrumentalist Company
      200 Northfield Road
      Northfield IL 60093

1235 Southwest Emblem Company
      P.O. Box 350
      Cisco TX 76437

1236 Trophyland USA, Inc.
      Dept. DM
      7001 W. 20th Avenue
      P.O. Box 4606
      Hialeah FL 33014

1237 United Musical Instruments
      1000 Industrial Parkway
      P.O. Box 727
      Elkhart IN 46515

Part 13
Twirling

The nation's largest baton twirling organizations are the United States Twirling Association (USTA) and the National Baton Twirling Association (NBTA). Both publish magazines. Twirl and Drum Major contain ads, rule changes, readers' comments, champion profiles—male and female—and contest schedules.

Like band competitions, many twirling contests (which are held indoors, the television movie Twirl notwithstanding) are won by the best people who show up. The USTA holds annual championships at different locations, while the NBTA's "America's Youth on Parade" annual championship is always held at Notre Dame University. The USTA has endeavored to have baton twirling recognized as a sport and discontinued the modeling portion of its contests.

Individual contest twirling has many categories—e.g., novice, intermediate, and advanced—which are further broken down by age and sometimes state. Group twirling, known as dance-twirl, parade corps, or corps, is usually performed to music selected by the unit's director, in contrast to solo twirling, which is often done to standard patriotic music.

In addition to the national twirling associations, group twirling is done by junior and senior high school squads in such organizations as the Cavalcade Indoor Drill Association (CIDA), which features twirlers in addition to color guards. Contests sponsored by the CIDA are geared for the spectators and judges in the bleachers, whereas in NBTA and USTA competitions, the soloists and small dance-twirl squads perform for a judge whose table is sometimes in the middle of the gym floor, obstructing the spectator's view.

A great deal of twirling is done on football fields each autumn by high school majorettes. "Majorette" is a term frowned upon by contest—and increasingly by all—twirlers but to a novice spectator only a hazy line separates the twirler from the majorette. Suffice it to say that all majorettes (not drum majorettes) are twirlers but not all twirlers are majorettes.

The January, February, and March 1980 issues of Twirl ran the series "Many Twirling Positions Are Available." Over a hundred colleges and universities were listed. Things change. Sometimes a corps-style band will eschew twirlers. Sometimes traditional "golden girls" remain. Sometimes inclusion in the band depends on the expertise of the twirler(s).

Associations

1238 Cavalcade Indoor Drill Association
c/o Robert Everitt
441 Bridge Street
Graterford PA 18944

1239 Drum Majorettes of America
5457 Wilkinson Blvd.
Charlotte NC 28208

1240 International Academy of
Twirling Teachers
300 S. Wright Road
Janesville WI 53545

1241 National Baton Twirling Association (NBTA)
Box 266
Janesville WI 53545

1242 United States Twirling Association (USTA)
P.O. Box 24488
Seattle WA 98124

1243 VFW
c/o Bob Brady, Chairman
National Marching Units and
Parade Committee
319 Tadmar Road
Ross Township
Perryville PA 15237

1244 World Federation of Baton
Twirling and Majorette Associations
P.O. Box 266
Janesville WI 53547

Baton Manufacturers and Distributors

1245 American Baton Company
P.O. Box 266
Janesville WI 53545

1246 The Jemm Company
3300 Walnut Street
Denver CO 80205

1247 Kraskin Batons
P.O. Box 156
12475 Xenwood Avenue So.
Savage MN 55378

1248 Starline Baton Company, Inc.
P.O. Box 5490
Pompano Beach FL 33074-5490

Costumes and Accessories

1249 Algy Costumes & Uniforms
440 N.E. 1st Avenue
Hallandale Fl 33009

1250 American Showbiz (Chet's)
Costume Fabric & Trim
Inc.

5347 NE Sandy Boulevard
Portland OR 97213

1251 Baums Inc.
106 South 11th Street
Philadelphia Pa 19107

Ridley High School Raider Marching Band, Folsom, Pennsylvania.

Marple-Newtown High School Symphonic Marching Band, Newtown Square, PA.

1252 Bernie Roe & Associates
P.O. Box 14852
Ithaca NY 14852
    Includes batons, trim

1253 Colorifics
P.O. Box 26657
Columbus OH 43226

1254 Cote Inc.
74 W. Bridge Street
Morrisville PA 19067

1255 Galaxy Enterprises, Inc.
6808 Laurel Bowie Road
Bowie MD 20715

1256 Leo's Dancewear Inc.
1900 N. Narragansett Avenue
Chicago IL 60639

1257 Taffy's on Parade
701 Beta Drive
Cleveland OH 44143

1258 Thompson Costume Trim
and Fabric
1232 SW 59th Street
Oklahoma City OK 73159

Western Majorette Supply *see*
American Showbiz (Chet's) Costume Fabric & Trim Inc.

1259 Wolff Fording Company
1187 Highland Avenue Nee
Boston MA

Selected Bibliography

Articles

1260 Barbian, Kathy. "Stretch Yourself to a Better Strutting Routine." *Twirl* (June/July/August 1978): 21.

1261 Campbell, Sharon. "Let's Talk About . . . Knee Injuries." *Twirl* (September/October 1981): 10.

1262 Cass, Julia. "Pity the Poor Twirling Girl." *Philadelphia Inquirer Today Magazine,* October 22, 1978, pp. 10–11.

1263 Coberley, Ron. "Twirling with the Band." *Twirl* (November 1980): 16.

1264 Elliott, Joseph E. "Tips on Buying Uniforms." *Instrumentalist* (August 1979): 39–41.

1265 Ewoldt, Karen. "Advice from a Graduate." *Drum Major* (July 1982): 9.

1266 Follett, Richard J. "What About the Majorettes?" *Instrumentalist* (October 1977): 57–59.

1267 "How to Buy School Band Uniforms." New York NY: National Association of Uniform Manufacturers.

1268 Howard, Diane. "Tips for School Twirlers." *Drum Major* (December 1980): 7.

1269 Humphrey, Elizabeth. "Baton Twirling: Discipline, Responsibility, Commitment." *Daily Local News* [West Chester PA] (July 12, 1987): A3.

1270 Kirkpatrick, Curry. "Calvin [Murphy] Discovers Murphy's Law." *Sports Illustrated* (August 15, 1977): 14-15.

1271 McCormack, Patricia. "Baton Twirling: An Unusual Route to College Scholarships." *Twirl* (November 1980): 13.

1272 March, Barbara M.; Nazario, Beth G.; and Moors, Susan D. "A Tribute to Terry Hopple." *Daily Local News* [West Chester PA] (November 20, 1987): 4.

1273 Moncure, Sue Swyrs. "U.D. Junior Becomes America's 'No. 1' Twirl Girl." *University of Delaware Update* (September 21, 1989): 3.

1274 Page, Nick. "Guide to Purchasing Band Uniforms." *Instrumentalist* (February 1988): 66, 68, 70-72.

1275 Pogue, Jan. "Lost in a Spin, A World Turns." *Philadelphia Inquirer* (October 18, 1981): 1B, 5B.

Mount Vernon High School Marching Majors, Mount Vernon, Virginia.

University of Delaware Blue Hen Marching Band with members of the 1984 Olympics marching band, Newark, Delaware.

1276 Portner, Robert. "How to Buy Band Uniforms." *American School and University* (July 1978): 44–47.

1277 Shields, Mike. "Twirling: Combination of Sport and Art Skills." *West Chester Citizen* (November 25, 1981): 1, 10.

1278 Verhulst, Jacob. "A Twirling Program." *Twirl* (February 1981): 21.

1279 Wareham, Duane E. "A Case for Majorettes." *Instrumentalist* (September 1959): 75–77, 91.

1280 Wolfe, Howard A. "Developing Trends in Band Uniforms." *School Musician, Director & Teacher* (November 1977): 48–49.

1281 Wurmstedt, Bob. "In Texas: Twirling to Beat the Band." *Time,* December 11, 1978, pp. 12, 16.

Books (Fiction)

1282 Lowry, Beverly. *Come Back, Lolly Ray.* Garden City NY: Doubleday, 1977.

Books (Nonfiction)

1283 Atwater, Constance. *Baton Twirling: The Fundamentals of an Art and a Skill.* Rutland VT, and Tokyo, Japan: Charles E. Tuttle Company, 1964.

1284 Davis, Roberta, Harriette Behringer and Doris Wheelus. *Cheerleading and Baton Twirling.* New York NY: Tempo Books, 1972.

1285 Hindsley, Mark H. *How to Twirl a Baton.* Chicago IL: Ludwig and Ludwig, 1928. Drum major baton/mace.

1286 Lee, Robert L. *The Baton: Twirling Made Easy!* New York NY: Boosey and Hawkes, 1949.

1287 Miller, Fred; Smith, Gloria; and Ardman, Perri. *The Complete Book of Baton Twirling.* Garden City NY: Doubleday, 1978.

1288 Orr, Susan Daily. *Baton Twirling Unlimited.* Indianapolis IN: Carl Hungness Publishing, 1981.

1289 Roberts, Bob. *The Twirler and the Twirling Corps.* New York NY: Carl Fischer, 1954.

1290 *Who's Who in Baton Twirling.* Janesville WI: National Baton Twirling Association, published annually.

Films

1291 *Twirl.* NBC Television movie, 1981.

Plays

1292 Martin, Jane. *Twirler. Esquire* (November 1982): 156–158.

General Bibliography

Articles

1293 Anderson, Robert. "Woodwind Crisis in Corps-Style Bands." *The Instrumentalist* (November 1982): 13.

1294 Bachman, Harold B. "The Case for the Marching Band." *Instrumentalist* (September 1959): 50-53.

1295 Bencriscutto, Frank A. "Let's Put It All Together." *The School Musician, Director & Teacher* (November 1979): 8-9.

1296 Bierley, Paul. "More Band History Needed." *Instrumentalist* (September 1992): 12.

1297 Blackford, R. Winston. "The Marching Band as a Musical Entity." *School Musician, Director & Teacher* (June/July 1978): 50-51.

1298 Blades, James. *Percussion Instruments and Their History.* Westport CT: Bold Strummer, 1993.

1299 Bocook, Jay. "Performing Corps-Style Music." *Instrumentalist* (June 1978): 32-33.

1300 Boullion, James L. "A Study of Music Performances at Athletic Contests." *School Musician, Director & Teacher* (March 1979): 46-48.

1301 Brammer, George. "A Primer on Sportslighting." *American School & University* (June 1987): 25-26, 30, 32.

1302 Branson, Branley A. "The Great Highland Pipes." *Instrumentalist* (October 1979): 23-25.

1303 "Brass Bands at Centre College." *Chronicle of Higher Education* (June 12, 1991): B5.

1304 Brazaukas, Paul. "Tips for Good Cymbal Playing." *Instrumentalist* (August 1982): 56, 58-59.

1305 Brion, Keith. "The 'Alternative' Marching Band." *Instrumentalist* (October 1977): 60-61.

1306 Cass, Julia. "High Stepping and Not for Half-Time Only." *Philadelphia Inquirer* (October 15, 1978): 1-A, 8-B.

1307 Castronovo, Albert J. "New Marching Sounds of the 80s." *School Musician, Director & Teacher* (August/September 1980): 8–9.

1308 Clayton, Nancy. "Battle of Flowers: Corps Style." *School Musician, Director & Teacher* (August/September 1981): 24–25.

1309 Clyne, Robert. "Memories of Marching on Liberty Weekend." *Instrumentalist* (January 1987): 71–74.

1310 Covert, Bob. "Easing the Transition from Traditional to Corps Style Marching." *Instrumentalist* (June 1981): 8–9.

1311 Cowherd, Ron. "Sousa Marches: The Arranged Versions." *Instrumentalist* (December 1977): 44–47.

1312 Davis, Oscar B. "Those Magnificent Marches." *School Musician, Director & Teacher* (June/July 1980): 10–11, 45.

1313 Day, Kingsley. "Music at the White House." *Instrumentalist* (August 1992): 38–40, 42, 60–61.

1314 De Leon, Erlinda A. "Letter: Support Our Bands." *Wilmington News-Journal* [DE] (January 11, 1988): A11.

1315 Dubois, John. "The Great Band Boom Marches On." *Philadelphia Bulletin* (October 10, 1978): 1, 5.

1316 Elliott, Robert. "The History of Bands from Jericho to Goldman." *Instrumentalist* (August 1992): 70–71.

1317 Evenson, E. Orville. "The March Style of Sousa." *Instrumentalist* (November 1954): 13–15, 48–50.

1318 "Everything's Fair Dinkum Down Under." *Instrumentalist* (August 1987): 54, 56, 58.

1319 Flor, Gloria J. "The 'Frumpet' and Other Marching Band Oddities." *School Musician, Director & Teacher* (August/September 1979): 24–25.

1320 Floyd, Robert. "No Pass/No Play—How Is Texas Faring?" *Instrumentalist* (April 1987): 33–34, 36.

1321 Garrison, Paul. "The Value of Marching Band." *Music Educators Journal* (January 1986): 48–52.

1322 Gasser, J.R., and Fred, B.G. "Bibliography of Marching Band, Baton Twirling, Flag Swinging, Gun Spinning, Drum and Bugle Corps." *Instrumentalist* Vol. I, No. 1 (September-October 1946): 15–17.

1323 Gerardi, J.L. "No Longer Football's Stepchild." *Instrumentalist* (June 1978): 28–29.

1324 "A High School Band with Bagpipes." *Instrumentalist* (October 1979): 25.

1325 Holmes, Kristin E. "A Grim Lesson and Sad Farewell: Victim [designer Bobby Hoffman] Reveals His AIDS for Students' Sake." *Philadelphia Inquirer* (October 24, 1990 [?]): 1, 7-A.

1326 Hoover, J. Douglas. "New Drums on an Old Budget." *School Musician, Director & Teacher* (August/September 1980): 10.

1327 Hoover, Jerry. "A Flip of the Coin." *Instrumentalist* (August 1982): 41.

1328 Houston, Bob. "Multiple Percussion on the March." *Instrumentalist* (May 1978): 32–35.

1329 "How Willingly We March: Directors Survey." *Instrumentalist* (December 1990): 18–23.

1330 "Is Marching Band in Step with Music Education?" *Music Educators Journal* (May 1985): 28–32.

1331 Jacobsen, James A. "The Responsibility of Music to Sports." *School Musician, Director & Teacher* (August/September 1981): 20–21.

1332 Johnson, William V. "Corps Style – Fad or Revolution?" *Instrumentalist* (June 1977): 22.

1333 Kastens, L. Kevin. "Achieving Musical Marching Band Performance." *Music Educators Journal* (September 1981): 26–29.

1334 Kohn, Jim. "The Play Just Won't Go Away." [Stanford, 1982] *Sports Illustrated* (November 21, 1988): 10.

1335 Lautzenheiser, Tim. "I Feel It!" *Instrumentalist* (October 1982): 30.

1336 Leckrone, Michael. "Simply Great – A Better Marching Band." *Music Educators Journal* (November 1987): 55–59.

1337 Lesinsky, Adam P. "Give the Girls a Chance." *School Musician, Director & Teacher* (August/September 1978): 60–61 (reprint from February 1930).

1338 Ludwig, W.F., Sr. "Sousa Had Rhythm." *School Musician, Director & Teacher* (October 1978): 78–79 (reprint from October 1935).

1339 Ludwig, William. "A History of American Drumming." *Instrumentalist* (November 1990): 22–26.

1340 McAllister, Robert L. "World's Largest Massed Band." *School Musician, Director & Teacher* (February 1979): 51–53 (reprint from November 1958).

1341 McMinn, Bill. "Small Marching Bands to the Fore." *Instrumentalist* (May 1988): 28–30, 33–34.

1342 "Making a List" [of college marching bands]. *Sports Illustrated* (October 7, 1991): 14.

1343 "Marching Bands at the Middle School Level?" *Music Educators Journal* (October 1990): 46–48.

1344 Mark, Michael, and Patten, Ansel. "Emergence of the Modern Marching Band (1950–1970)." *Instrumentalist* (June 1976): 33–36.

1345 Middendorf, J. William. "The Drums Go 'Bang' and the Cymbals 'Clang.'" *Saturday Evening Post* (October 1976): 64–65, 78.

1346 Milbank, Dana. "Marching Bands Clean Up Their Acts or Just Pretend To." *Wall Street Journal* (December 26, 1991): 1, A4.

1347 Mitchell, Dave. "Corps vs. Traditional: A Comparison of Marching Styles and Values." *School Musician, Director & Teacher* (August/September 1980): 6–7.

1348 Mufson, Steve. "Ivy League Bands Keep on Marching to X-Rated Tunes." *Wall Street Journal* (September 25, 1981): 1, 19.

1349 Neilson, James. "The High School Marching Band." *School Musician, Director & Teacher* (April 1981): 12–13.

1350 Nelson, Judy Ruppel. "Gene Thrailkill — Guiding the Pride." [University of Oklahoma] *Instrumentalist* (September 1987): 17–19.

1351 Pedigo, Dwayne L. "Electronics in the Marching Band — A Sound New Sound Dimension." *Instrumentalist* (June 1980): 10–11.

1352 Poe, Gerald. "The Marching Band: More Than 'Just Music.'" *School Musician, Director & Teacher* (August/September 1978): 70.

1353 Rapp, Willis. "The Evolution of Multi-Toms." *Percussionist* (Spring/Summer 1980): 132–139.

1354 Revelli, William D. "Marching Is an Educational Plus." *School Musician, Director & Teacher* (August/September 1979): 8–9, 60–61.

1355 Rideout, Roger R. "Summer Tasks for the First-Year Band Director." *Instrumentalist* (July 1987): 50, 52, 54.

1356 Salatto, Art. "Great Valley's Music Parents Assn. Drums Up Support for Band Students." *Suburban Advertiser* [PA] (September 17, 1987): 19.

1357 Salzman, Tom. "A Marching Wind Ensemble." *Instrumentalist* (May 1985): 88, 90.

1358 Skilton, John M. "Some Items to Consider When Selecting a Music School Next Year." *Drum Corps News* (March 25, 1983): 15.

1359 Smith, Jack W. "An Alternate to the Marching Band." *School Musician, Director & Teacher* (January 1980): 8–9, 47.

1360 Snupp, Kenneth. "Corps Style Marching: A Blessing or a Curse?" *School Musician, Director & Teacher* (May 1980): 6, 13.

1361 "Steppin' Out at Stanford." *Oui* (November 1978): 94(5).

1362 Stock, Robert. "Bands on the March." *New York Times Magazine* (July 4, 1982): 12–15, 27, 33.

1363 Sullivan, Robert. "Pianissimo, but Con Gusto." [Columbia University] *Sports Illustrated* (October 13, 1986): 17.

1364 Tuttle, David R. "Band—Take the Field." [University of Michigan in Rose Bowl] *Instrumentalist* (March 1965): 51–53.

1365 Vigoda, Ralph. "John Philip Sousa Just Isn't Enough." *Philadelphia Inquirer* (October 12, 1993): B1, B2.

1366 Wanamaker, Jay. "George H. Tuthill: A Pioneer in Marching Percussion." *School Musician, Director & Teacher* (August/September 1981): 22–23.

1367 _____. "The Olympic All-American Marching Band." *Instrumentalist* (January 1985): 37–40.

1368 _____. "Survey of Marching Percussion Materials." *Instrumentalist* (September 1980): 84, 86–89.

1369 Waybright, David. "Brass Playing in the Marching Band." *Instrumentalist* (June 1984): 12–13.

1370 White, Jack W. "Corps-Style Rehearsals." *Instrumentalist* (June 1978): 30–31.

1371 Wilhjelm, Christian, and Rife, Jerry. "The Sousa Band Centennial." *Instrumentalist* (December 1992): 46, 48–50, 53–54.

Books

1372 Bierley, Paul E. *John Philip Sousa, American Phenomenon,* rev. ed. Westerville OH: Integrity Press, 1992.

1373 Binion, T., Jr. *High School Marching Band.* Englewood Cliffs NJ: Prentice-Hall, 1973.

1374 Bollinger, Donald E. *Band Directors Complete Handbook.* Englewood Cliffs NJ: Prentice-Hall, 1979.

1375 Chase, Gilbert. *America's Music: From the Pilgrims to the Present.* 3rd ed. Champaign IL: University of Illinois Press, 1987.

1376 Duvall, W. Clyde. *The High School Band Director's Handbook.* Englewood Cliffs NJ: Prentice-Hall, 1960.

1377 Foster, Robert E. *Multiple-Option Marching Band Techniques.* 3rd ed. Port Washington NY: Alfred Publishing, 1992. Includes history of marching bands.

1378 Goldman, Edwin Franko. *Band Betterment: Suggestions and Advice to Bands, Bandmasters, and Band-Players.* New York NY: Carl Fischer, 1934.

1379 Hazen, Margaret Hindle, and Hazen, Robert M. *The Music Men: An Illustrated History of Brass Bands in America, 1800–1920.* Washington DC: Smithsonian Institution Press, 1987.

1380 Herbert, T., ed. *Bands: The Brass Band Movement in the 19th and 20th Centuries.* Buckingham, England: Open University Press, 1991.

1381 Hertz, Wayne S., ed. *Music in the Senior High School.* MENC Music in American Life Commission VI. Washington DC: Music Educators National Corporation, 1959.

1382 Hjelmervik, Kenneth, and Berg, Richard. *Marching Bands.* New York NY: A.S. Barnes, 1953.

1383 Hong, Sherman, and Hamilton, Jim. *Percussion Section: Developing the Corps Style.* Petal MS: Band Shed, 1978.

1384 Kraus, David. *A Visible Feast.* Lawrence KS: University of Kansas, 1980.

1385 Loken, Newt, and Dypwick, Otis. *Cheerleading & Marching Bands.* New York NY: A.S. Barnes, 1945.

1386 Mercer, R. Jack. *The Band Director's Brain Bank.* Evanston IL: Instrumentalist, 1970.

1387 Neidig, Kenneth L. *The Band Director's Guide.* Englewood Cliffs NJ: Prentice-Hall, 1964.

1388 Pavlakis, Christopher. *The American Music Handbook.* New York NY: Free Press, 1974.

1389 Probasco, Jim. *A Parent's Guide to Band and Orchestra.* Foreword by Tom Batiuk. White Hall and Crozet VA: Betterway Publications, 1991.

1390 Righter, Charles B. *Gridiron Pageantry: The Story of the Marching Band for Bandsmen, Directors and Football Fans.* Cooper Square NY: Carl Fischer, 1941.

1391 Scott, Willard. *America Is My Neighborhood.* New York: Simon & Schuster, 1987. Includes section on Dr. William P. Foster of Florida A&M University, author of *Band Pageantry.*

1392 Shellahamer, Bentley; Swearingen, James; and Woods, Jon. *The Marching Band Program: Principles and Practices.* Oskaloosa IA: C.L. Barnhouse, 1986.

1393 Sousa, John Philip. *Marching Along.* Boston MA: Hale, Cushman and Flint, 1928.

1394 Wells, James R. *The Marching Band in Contemporary Music Education.* New York NY: Interland Publishing, 1976.

1395 Whitwell, David. *A New History of Wind Music.* Evanston IL: Instrumentalist, 1972.

Periodicals

An attempt has been made to include only those magazines relevant to marching activities. Magazines like High Fidelity *and* Stereo Review *could be of use for locating reviews of records, tapes, and compact discs.*

1396 Accent on Music (formerly Accent)
Accent Publications
12100 W. 6th Avenue
Box 15337
Denver CO 80215

1397 American Music
University of Illinois Press
54 E. Gregory Drive
Champaign IL 61820

1398 The American Music Teacher
Music Teachers National Association
617 Vine Street, Suite 1432
Cincinnati OH 45202-2434

1399 Bandworld
407 Terrace Street
Ashland OR 97520
Published January, March,
May, August, November by
Western International Band
Clinic

1400 BDGuide
Village Press, Inc.
2779 Aero Park Drive
Traverse City MI 49684
Published bimonthly during
school year

1401 Brass Quarterly
Published 1957–1964

1402 CBDNA Journal
College Band Directors National Association
Box 8028
Austin TX 78767

1403 The Clarinet
P.O. Box 450622
Atlanta GA 30345-0622

1404 DCI Today
(Drum Corps International)
P.O. Box 548
Lombard IL 60148-0548

1405 Drum Corps News
Ceased publication

1406 Drum Corps World
P.O. Box 8052
Madison WI 53708-8052

1407 Drum Major Magazine
National Baton Twirling Association

Box 266
Janesville WI 53545

1408 Electronic Music Educator
200 Northfield Road
Northfield IL 60093

1409 Flute Talk
Instrumentalist Company
200 Northfield Road
Northfield IL 60093

1410 High Fidelity
Ceased publication

1411 The Horn Call
International Horn Society
School of Arts and Letters
Southeast Oklahoma State
University
Durant OK 74701

1412 Instrumentalist
200 Northfield Road
Northfield IL 60093

1413 Journal of Band Research
Troy State University Press
Troy AL 36082

1414 Marching Bands & Corps
River City Publications
P.O. Box 8341
Jacksonville FL 32211
Ceased publication

1415 Modern Drummer
Modern Drummer Publications
870 Pompton Avenue
Cedar Grove NJ 07009

1416 Modern Percussionist
P.O. Box 469
Cedar Grove NJ 07009

1417 Music & Pageantry Journal
One issue; ceased publication

1418 Music Educators Journal
Music Educators National
Conference
1902 Association Drive
Reston VA 22091

1419 Music Journal
Ceased publication 1985

1420 On Parade
All American Association of
Contest Judges
1627 Lay Boulevard
Kalamazoo MI 49001

1421 Percussive Notes
Percussive Arts Society
214 West Main St.
P.O. Box 697
Urbana IL 61801-0697
Includes ongoing section,
"Percussion on the March"

1422 School Musician, Director &
Teacher
Ammark Publishing Com-
pany

4049 W. Peterson
Chicago IL 60646
Ceased publication 1987

1423 Starting Line
1830 Toombs Drive
Akron OH 44306
Drum corps

1424 Stereo Review
Hachette Filipacchi Maga-
zines, Inc.
1633 Broadway
New York NY 10019

1425 Today's Music Educator
P.O. Box 8052
Madison WI 53708
Published February and Sep-
tember by Drum Corps
Sights & Sounds, Inc.

1426 Twirl Magazine
U.S. Twirling Association
P.O. Box 24488
Seattle WA 98124

Index

References are to entry numbers, not pages.